QUICK & EASY
Sewing
FOR CHRISTMAS™

Edited by Vicki Blizzard

HOUSE of
WHITE
BIRCHES
PUBLISHERS
SINCE 1947

Quick & Easy Sewing for Christmas

Editor: Vicki Blizzard
Associate Editors: Kelly Keim, Barb Sprunger
Technical Editor: Mary Jo Kurten
Copy Editors: Mary Nowak, Nicki Lehman
Technical Artists: Leslie Brandt, Julie Catey, Jessica Rothe, Chad Summers
Publication Coordinator: Tanya Turner

Photography: Tammy Christian, Jeff Chilcote, Justin P. Wiard
Photography Stylist: Arlou Wittwer
Photography Assistant: Linda Quinlan

Production Coordinator: Brenda Gallmeyer
Book and Cover Design: Jessi Butler
Production Artist: Ronda Bechinski
Production Assistants: Janet Bowers, Marj Morgan
Traffic Coordinator: Sandra Beres

Publishers: Carl H. Muselman, Arthur K. Muselman
Chief Executive Officer: John Robinson
Marketing Director: Scott Moss
Book Marketing Manager: Craig Scott
Product Development Director: Vivian Rothe
Publishing Services Manager: Brenda R. Wendling

Printed in Italy
First Printing: 2001
Library of Congress Number: 00-109648
ISBN: 1-882138-73-2

FROM THE EDITOR

What's the one thing we all wish we had more of, especially around the holiday season? Time, of course! With all the hustle and bustle of preparation and celebration, time is the precious commodity we all run out of before we're finished with everything we need to do.

With that in mind, we've gathered together a large assortment of designs for quick-to-stitch projects that are just perfect for Christmas gift giving. From ornaments to wearables, we've tried to include something for everyone on your gift list.

Each of the wonderful projects in this book can be stitched in a matter of a few hours by those with average sewing skills. In a few evenings or a weekend, you can easily complete gifts for everyone on your list, from your sister to your friend at work to the mailman. And just imagine their happy surprise when they open a package containing something made with love just for them!

Keep your pen and paper handy while you're browsing through this book— I know you'll want to jot down notes of that just-right present for each name on your list!

Warm regards,

Vicki Blizzard

CONTENTS

Tiny Treasures

Holly Jolly Accents

Santa's Workshop

Fun & Fancy

Stitched With Love

All Decked Out

TINY TREASURES

Standing ready to delight you with every turn of the page, our collection of little goodies is ready to be sewn quickly for package tie-ons or holiday ornaments.

Snowmen abound, as do snowflakes and ice crystal ornaments. Our little angel pin will amuse you while you sew her and will make the lucky recipient smile as she opens the package. Be sure to "cook up" a batch of quick-to-stitch gingerbread ornaments to give to all your friends who love to bake!

Keep a basket of these treasures handy to give away to visitors as they share in your holiday festivities!

FLUFFY SNOWMEN

By Phyllis M. Dobbs

This trio is cute, snuggly, warm and wonderful as well as quick-to-make and perfect to give.

Project Specifications

Skill Level: Beginner
Ornament Sizes: Approximately 4½" x 5¾", 3¾" x 7¾" and 4¼" x 6¼"

Materials

Note: Materials and instructions are for set of three snowmen.

- White chenille fabric 8" x 28" or 18" x 14"
- Glass pebble beads for buttons: 4 each ruby and bottle green and 6 black
- 3 orange oval beads for noses
- 6 (4mm) black cabochons for eyes
- 3 plaid fabric strips 1" x 12"
- Polyester fiberfill
- ⅔ yard ⅛"-wide green satin ribbon
- White all-purpose thread
- Jewel glue
- Basic sewing supplies and tools

Instructions

Step 1. Trace and cut snowmen as directed on patterns.

Step 2. On front piece of each snowman and referring to photo for placement, sew beads for buttons and noses.

Step 3. Cut ⅛"-wide green satin ribbon in three 8" lengths. Pin ends of each ribbon to top center of each snowman's head with loop of ribbon hanging down the front of snowman.

Step 4. Pin right sides of each snowman together, with ribbon hanger between the two pieces. Stitch with ¼" seam allowance, leaving a 1½" opening along bottom edge.

Step 5. Turn right side out, stuff with polyester fiberfill and stitch opening closed.

Step 6. Fringe ½" on each end of plaid fabric strips and tie around neck of each snowman.

Step 7. Glue two black cabochons to each face for eyes. ❄

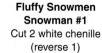

Fluffy Snowmen
Snowman #1
Cut 2 white chenille
(reverse 1)

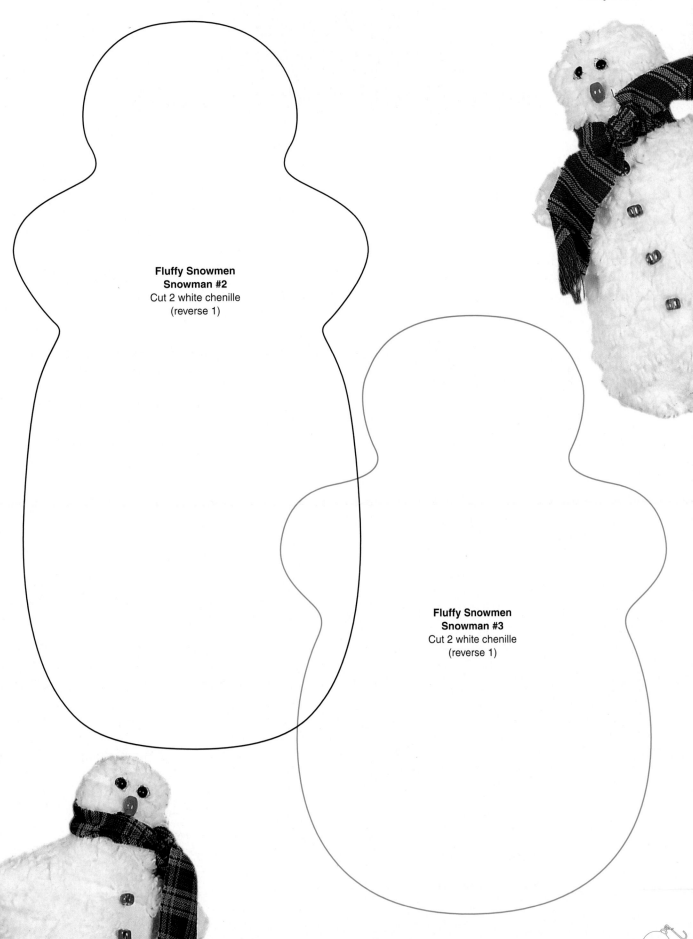

**Fluffy Snowmen
Snowman #2**
Cut 2 white chenille
(reverse 1)

**Fluffy Snowmen
Snowman #3**
Cut 2 white chenille
(reverse 1)

EASY CUTWORK SNOWFLAKE ORNAMENTS

By Karen Neary

Create your own snow flurry with these remarkably pretty, but fast and easy snowflakes.

Project Specifications

Skill Level: Beginner
Snowflake Size: Approximately 4" x 4"

Materials

Note: Materials and directions are for one snowflake.

- 2 squares 5" x 5" white-on-white fabric
- 2 squares 5" x 5" medium-weight fusible interfacing
- 5" x 5" square fusible transfer web
- 5" x 5" square tear-away stabilizer
- Permanent marker
- Sharp embroidery scissors
- Metallic silver machine sewing thread
- Basic sewing supplies and tools

Instructions

Step 1. Apply medium-weight fusible interfacing to wrong sides of white fabric squares following manufacturer's instructions.

Step 2. Apply fusible transfer web to wrong side of one interfaced square. Remove paper backing and fuse to wrong side of other interfaced square.

Step 3. Trace snowflake pattern of your choice onto tear-away stabilizer using permanent marker. Pin to right side of prepared fabric square. Stitch on pattern lines using metallic silver thread in machine.

Step 4. When stitching is complete, carefully remove tear-away stabilizer. Using sharp embroidery scissors, cut excess fabric away between stitching lines and around outside edges.

Step 5. Cut a 12" length of silver metallic thread. Attach to snowflake for hanging loop. ✺

Patterns continued on page 12

Cutwork Snowflake #1

Cutwork Snowflake #2

GINGERBREAD ORNAMENTS

By Phyllis M. Dobbs

Dress them up in holiday finery and hang these spicy little ornaments on the tree, tie them to boxes or tuck them in just for fun.

Project Specifications
Skill Level: Beginner
Ornament Size: Approximately 4" x 5½"

Materials
Note: Materials and instructions for set of two ornaments.

- Brown felt 6" x 18"
- Green felt 4" x 12"
- 2 (¾") ceramic bow buttons
- 15 red silver-lined rochaille beads
- 1 (½") red heart bead
- Polyester fiberfill
- 16" (⅛"-wide) red satin ribbon
- 4 (4mm) black cabochons for eyes
- All-purpose green sewing thread
- Jewel glue
- Basic sewing supplies and tools

Instructions
Step 1. Trace and cut felt as directed on patterns.

Step 2. Referring to photo for placement, sew ceramic bow buttons to each of two brown felt body fronts and heart bead to front of dress.

Step 3. For the lady ornament place dress over a body front and a body back. Stitch around periphery of body, including dress, leaving 1" opening near top of head. Stuff lightly with polyester fiberfill. Cut an 8" length of ⅛"-wide red satin ribbon, enclose ends in head opening and sew to close. Sew seven red silver-lined rochaille beads along bottom edge of dress.

Step 4. For man ornament place vest front pieces over body front, then layer over body back and vest back. Stitch, stuff and finish as in Step 3. Sew four red silver-lined rochaille beads along each vest edge.

Step 5. Glue black cabochons to face for eyes. ✾

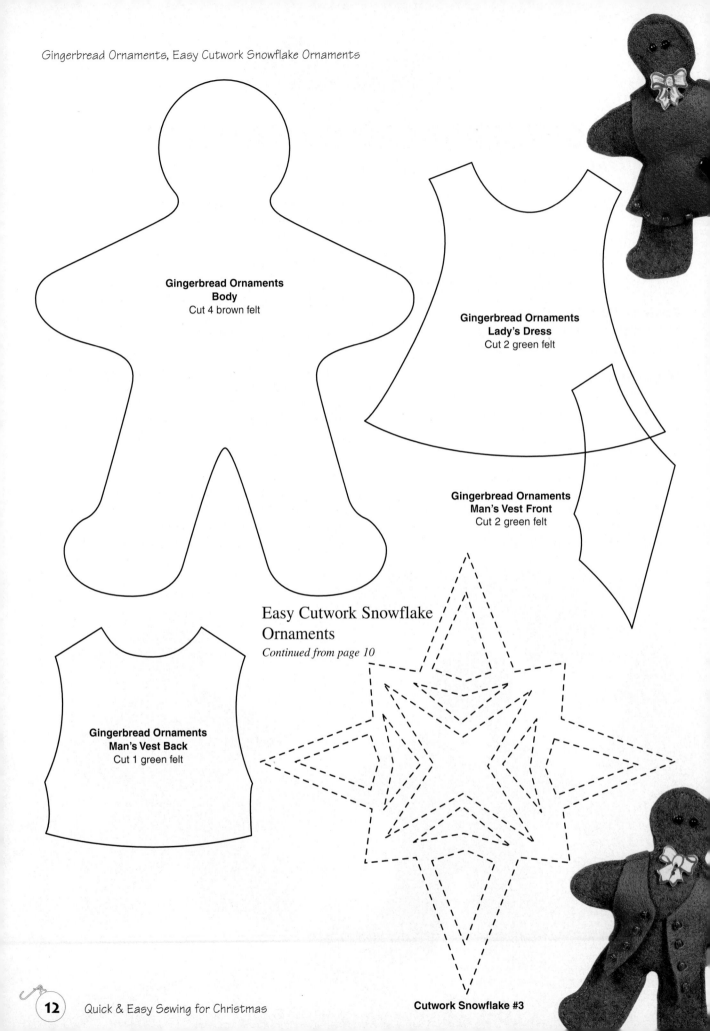

**Gingerbread Ornaments
Body**
Cut 4 brown felt

**Gingerbread Ornaments
Lady's Dress**
Cut 2 green felt

**Gingerbread Ornaments
Man's Vest Front**
Cut 2 green felt

Easy Cutwork Snowflake Ornaments
Continued from page 10

**Gingerbread Ornaments
Man's Vest Back**
Cut 1 green felt

Cutwork Snowflake #3

ICE CRYSTAL ORNAMENT

By Mary Ayres

A silvery, shimmery delight to hang on the tree or make a package very special.

Project Specifications
Skill Level: Beginner
Ornament Size: Approximately 3" x 7½"

Materials
- Scrap of textured blue fabric 4" x 8"
- Scrap of textured white fabric 3" x 3"
- Scrap of fusible web 3" x 3"
- ½ yard iridescent white medium rickrack
- White 3½" tassel
- ½ yard ½"-wide wired silver ribbon
- Silver metallic pearl cotton
- 1 (⅝") flat silver button
- Embroidery needle
- All-purpose thread to match fabrics
- Paper sachet or polyester fiberfill
- Basic sewing supplies and tools

Instructions
Note: Use ¼" seam allowance unless otherwise indicated.

Step 1. Cut two 3½" circles from textured blue fabric for front and back of ornament.

Step 2. Trace snowflake on paper side of fusible transfer web. Fuse to back of textured white fabric following manufacturer's directions. Cut out on traced solid lines.

Step 3. Position snowflake on center of front blue circle. Fuse in place. Mark stitching details on snowflake and blue circle. Using silver metallic pearl cotton, work buttonhole

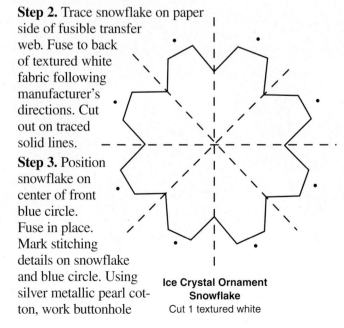

**Ice Crystal Ornament
Snowflake**
Cut 1 textured white

stitch around outside edge of snowflake and embroider stem stitch along stitching lines. Make a French knot at each dot, wrapping pearl cotton once around needle for each knot. Sew silver button to center of snowflake with silver metallic pearl cotton.

Step 4. Sew rickrack around circle front ¼" from edge, beginning and ending at center top and sewing through center of rickrack. Cut a 5" piece of rickrack for hanging loop. Fold in half and baste raw edges to center top of circle front.

Step 5. With right sides together, sew front and back circles together along rickrack stitching, leaving 1" open for turning.

Step 6. Turn ornament right side out. Fill with paper sachet or polyester fiberfill. Sew opening closed.

Step 7. Sew top of tassel to center bottom of ornament. Tie silver ribbon in a bow. Trim bow ends even and sew to center top of ornament. Shape bow attractively. ❄

ANGEL GARLAND

By Chris Malone

Seven lovable little guardian angels to grace your window, door or mantel. Hallelujah!

Project Specifications

Skill Level: Beginner

Angel Size: Approximately 6" x 5"

Garland Size: Approximately 6" x 48"

Materials

- ¼ yard unbleached muslin
- 4 red prints and 3 green prints 6" x 11" each
- Thin cotton batting 12" x 15"
- Natural, red, green, light brown and black all-purpose threads
- Kraft paper or recycled brown grocery bag
- 14 (3mm) black beads
- 13" light brown wool roving for hair
- 7 (1") grapevine hearts
- 8 (2") grapevine wreaths
- 6 (1") grapevine bows
- ⅔ yard ⅛"-wide red satin ribbon
- ½ yard ⅛"-wide green satin ribbon
- ½ yard 1"-wide green grosgrain ribbon
- 80" mini boxwood garland
- Polyester fiberfill
- Powdered blush
- Cotton-tip swab
- Glue gun and glue sticks
- Basic sewing supplies and tools

Instructions

Note: Instructions are for one angel. Repeat for three angels in green dresses and four angels in red dresses.

Step 1. Trace angel head/arms on unbleached muslin. Pin traced angel to second piece of muslin. Stitch on traced lines, leaving open at bottom. Cut out ⅛" from stitched line. Clip curves and turn right side out. Stuff firmly with polyester fiberfill and sew opening closed.

Step 2. Trace and cut dress as directed on pattern. Pin pieces together, right sides facing, and sew a ¼" seam, leaving open at top and at each side where indicated on pattern. Clip curves and turn right side out. Fold and press a ⅜" hem at top of dress and press in ¼" seam

allowance at arm openings. Lightly stuff bottom of dress with polyester fiberfill.

Step 3. Starting at center back, hand-sew gathering stitches around neck, ¼" from fold. Insert bottom of head/arms into dress, slipping arms through side sleeve holes. Pull gathers so dress fits snugly around neck; take a few stitches into neck to secure, knot and clip thread.

Step 4. Trace wings on brown paper. Rough-cut about ½" from traced lines. Place paper, traced lines up, on wrong side of cotton batting. Tape or pin paper to batting on outside margin of paper. Thread machine with light brown thread and sew on traced lines. Cut out wings about ⅛" from stitching.

Step 5. With black thread, sew two black beads to face for eyes, knotting ends of thread at top head seam, which will be covered with hair. Apply powdered blush to cheeks with cotton-tip swab.

Step 6. For hair, cut wool roving into 1¾" length. Pull to remove strings and tie a knot in center of length. Gently pull roving on either side of knot to spread and fluff, leaving hair tight at ends. Glue knot to top of head. Apply a small amount of glue to sides of head and press hair to head.

Step 7. Cut red and green ⅛"-wide satin ribbon into

6" lengths. Wrap each piece around the center section of a grapevine heart, tie a bow and trim ends. Glue hearts to front neck edge of angels, matching ribbon color to dress.

Step 8. Apply a line of glue down center of wings, on batting side, and press to back of angel.

Step 9. Cut mini boxwood garland into eight 10" lengths. Spiral-wrap each piece around a grapevine wreath. Glue grapevine bows to six wreaths, covering

Continued on page 30

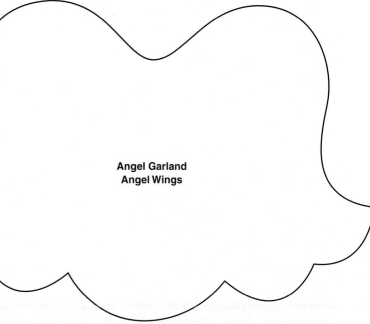

Angel Garland
Angel Wings

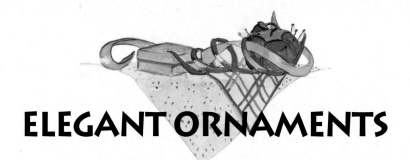

ELEGANT ORNAMENTS

By Donna Friebertshauser

These four perfectly beautiful ornaments can be used together as a set, but each, individually, stands on its own merit.

Project Specifications
Skill Level: Beginner
Ornament Size: Each approximately 4" x 4"

Materials

For Round Ornament
- Red felt 6½" x 6½"
- 1 package ¾"-wide white pre-ruffled lace
- 1 package ½" round lace medallions
- ½ yard (⅛") white pre-strung beads
- 6" (¹⁄₁₆"-wide) red satin ribbon
- 32 white seed beads

For Inverted Heart Ornament
- Red felt 7½" x 7½"
- 2 yards (⅛") pre-strung white beads
- 1 package ⅜"-wide white braid

For Bell Ornament
- White felt 8" x 8"
- 1 package gold metallic rickrack
- 6" metallic gold soutache or other gold braid
- 6-strand gold metallic embroidery thread
- 12 gold seed beads.
- Small piece of lightweight cardboard

For Inverted Teardrop Ornament
- White felt 6" x 9"
- 1 spool each red and green ribbon floss or silk ribbon
- 1 skein red rayon floss
- 1 package (⅜") gold bugle beads
- 1 package each red, green and gold seed beads
- 6" (⅛"-wide) white satin ribbon

For All Ornaments
- Red and white all-purpose thread
- #7 embroidery needle and #10 beading or embroidery needle
- Basic sewing supplies and tools

Instructions

ROUND ORNAMENT

Step 1. Trace and cut felt as directed on template.

Step 2. Place five round lace medallions near both outer edges of each red felt circle as shown on pattern. Stitch in place by hand with white thread. Anchor knot so it will not be visible when ornament is assembled.

Step 3. Between each medallion sew a white seed bead as indicated on pattern. Stitch with white thread. To attach firmly bring needle up from back of circle, go through bead and back down into felt. Right next to where needle exited, insert needle again from the back and go through the same bead from the other direction and down to the back again. Take a small stitch under the bead before proceeding to the next bead. Repeat for all pieces.

Step 4. When all four pieces have been embellished place two together with wrong sides facing. Insert pre-ruffled lace between felt pieces and sew together using red thread. Repeat with second two pieces.

Step 5. Place one completed piece on top of another completed piece and sew together by stitching down the center as indicated on pattern by hand or by machine.

Step 6. Cut three lengths of pre-strung beads each 5". Fold in half. With white thread attach the folded section of the beads to one end of the ball. Sew securely in place, carefully concealing white thread in edge of red felt.

Step 7. Fold red satin ribbon in half and attach ends at top of circle for hanger.

INVERTED HEART ORNAMENT

Step 1. Trace and cut hearts as directed on template.

Step 2. Place white braid at center of heart point and follow placement design on pattern. Insert a loop of pre-strung white beads within the braid loop. (Measure and cut each length of beads separately as loops may vary slightly in size.) Stitch beads and braid in place with white thread. Anchor securely on wrong side with knot. Tuck end of braid under top braid to conceal raw end. Repeat for each section.

Step 3. Place two hearts wrong sides together. Whip together by hand with small stitches using red thread. Repeat with second pair of hearts.

Step 4. Place one completed heart on top of the other and sew together by hand or machine from the cleft to the point.

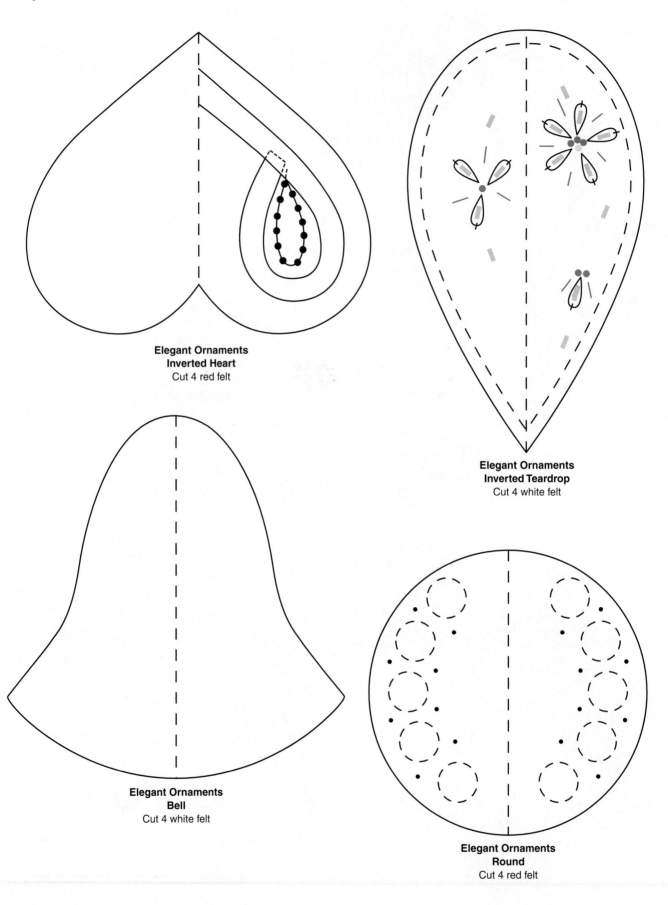

Elegant Ornaments
Inverted Heart
Cut 4 red felt

Elegant Ornaments
Inverted Teardrop
Cut 4 white felt

Elegant Ornaments
Bell
Cut 4 white felt

Elegant Ornaments
Round
Cut 4 red felt

Step 5. Starting at heart point attach pre-strung beads to outer edge of each segment. Sew securely between each bead with red thread.

Step 6. Cut four lengths of pre-strung beads 5" long. Fold in half. With white thread attach the folded section of the beads to one end of the ball. Sew securely in place, carefully concealing white thread in edge of red felt.

Step 7. Loop a 5" length of pre-strung beads in half and sew ends securely to point of heart for hanger.

BELL ORNAMENT

Step 1. Trace and cut bells as directed on template.

Step 2. With one strand of gold metallic embroidery thread work 13–15 star stitches as shown in Fig. 1 at random on each bell shape. Angle and scatter stars.

Step 3. Place two bells together wrong sides facing. Repeat with second pair of bells.

Fig. 1
Star Stitch

Step 4. Starting at top of bell, insert gold rickrack between bell layers with points only showing beyond edges of felt. With white thread whip two bell pieces together with small hand stitches. It works best to insert small sections of rickrack as you sew, folding or pleating at corners.

Step 5. Place one bell on top of the other and sew together from top to bottom by hand or machine.

Step 6. To make tassel, cut a piece of lightweight cardboard 1½" x 3". Thread a needle with a 12" length of gold metallic embroidery thread and set aside.

Step 7. Wrap gold metallic embroidery thread around 2½" width of cardboard 20 or more times. Insert threaded needle under top portion of wraps. Tie a half knot. Do not cut the loops of the tassel.

Step 8. Bring needle thread down along wrapped threads and wind it around the bundle of threads to form a ball or head of the tassel. Securely wrap several times to form a collar. Bring the needle from the bottom of the collar back up through the head. This completes the tassel. Attach to bottom of the bell with gold metallic thread.

Step 9. Cut loops and trim tassel.

Step 10. Sew loop of soutache or other braid to top of bell for hanger. Sew gold seed beads to ends of braid to conceal raw edges.

INVERTED TEARDROP ORNAMENT

Step 1. Trace and cut ovals as directed on template.

Step 2. With one strand of red rayon floss work a series of running stitches ⅜" from edges of felt ovals.

Step 3. Refer to pattern for placement of embroidered flowers. Flowers are stitched with lazy-daisy stitches using red silk ribbon or ribbon floss, each approximately ⅜" in length as shown in Fig. 2. Keep ribbon flat and relaxed as the stitch is worked.

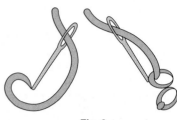

Fig. 2
Lazy-Daisy Stitch

Step 4. Centers of large and medium flowers each have three French knots. The single bud has only two French knots. Do not carry ribbon from one flower to another as shadow will show on front.

Step 5. In the center of each lazy-daisy stitch sew a gold bugle bead using white thread. Come up inside a petal, through the bead and down to the back. Move the needle slightly away and come up and through the bead in the other direction.

Step 6. Sew five bugle beads above and below flowers. Refer to pattern for placement.

Step 7. Work small green straight ribbon stitches between petals to represent leaves. Refer to pattern for placement.

Step 8. Place two oval sections wrong sides together. With white thread and small stitches whip the two pieces together. Repeat with second pair of ovals.

Step 9. Place one oval on top of the other and sew together from top to point by hand or machine. Finish edges by alternating a gold bugle bead with a gold seed bead. Use white thread to stitch to oval edges.

Step 10. String six gold bugle beads alternately with six gold seed beads. At the end add two red seed beads and one green seed bead as shown in Fig. 3. Bring the needle back up through the beads to point of oval. Continue to string tassels of slightly varying lengths for a total of seven. Knot to secure.

Step 11. Fold white satin ribbon in half and attach ends at top of oval for hanger. ✽

Fig. 3
String beads as shown.

HALLELUJAH ANGEL PIN

By Karen Mead

Wear with good spirit during the joyful holiday season this symbol of sweetness, innocence
and love.

Project Specifications
Skill Level: Beginner
Pin Size: Approximately 3¼" x 5½"

Materials
- 4" x 8" scrap of green fabric
- 3" x 3" square of beige linen or muslin
- 3 tiny twigs
- Jewelry pin closure for back
- Fine-line black permanent marker
- Removable marker
- 2 (⅜") buttons
- Powdered blush
- Cotton-tip swab
- All-purpose threads to match fabrics
- Clear spray acrylic sealer
- Polyester fiberfill
- Craft tacky glue
- Green, red, beige and dark yellow 6-strand embroidery floss
- Embroidery needle
- Basic sewing supplies and tools

Instructions
Note: Use ¼" seam allowance unless otherwise indicated.

Step 1. Trace and cut materials as directed on patterns.

Step 2. For angel front, stitch head to body, right sides facing; press seam up. Repeat for angel back.

Step 3. Referring to Fig. 1 trace face and halo onto angel face with removable marker. When satisfied with features, trace eyelids and fill in mouth with fine-line black permanent marker.

Step 4. With one strand of green embroidery floss straight-stitch halo and add lazy-daisy stitches (see page 19) for leaves. With one strand of red embroidery floss work French knots for berries. Sew two buttons to front of angel dress.

Step 5. Trace "Hallelujah" and three stars to front of dress, referring to Fig. 1. With one strand of beige embroidery floss embroider word with simple straight stitch. Embroider stars with dark yellow embroidery floss in straight stitch.

Continued on page 31

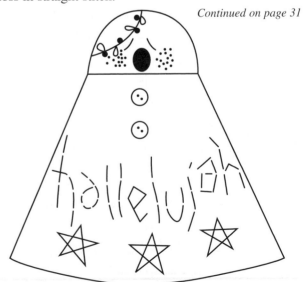

Fig. 1
Face, halo and stitching placement.

BUTTONED-UP ORNAMENTS

By Mary Ayres

These bright ornaments are primitive in style, but right up-to-date trimmed with glitzy gold metallic thread.

Project Specifications

Skill Level: Beginner
Ornament Size: Approximately 3" in diameter

Materials

- Scraps of blue, gold, red, purple, green, teal and brown felt or wool
- Gold metallic pearl cotton
- Embroidery needle
- Scraps of polyester fiberfill
- 3 (¾") flat brown buttons
- Basic sewing supplies and tools

Instructions

STAR

Step 1. Cut two 3" circles from blue wool or felt. Trace and cut star as directed on pattern and pin to one blue circle.

Step 2. Work buttonhole stitch around outside edge of appliqué with gold metallic pearl cotton. Sew a brown button to center of appliqué with gold metallic pearl cotton.

Step 3. Pin appliquéd circle to second circle. Work buttonhole stitch around edge with gold metallic pearl cotton, hiding knots inside circle. Leave 1" opening for stuffing (do not cut pearl cotton). Fill circles lightly with polyester fiberfill. Continue buttonhole stitching to close opening. Knot to secure.

Step 4. Cut a 10" piece of gold metallic pearl cotton. Run pearl cotton through buttonhole stitch at center top of ornament and knot ends together for hanger.

Buttoned-Up Ornaments
Star
Cut 1 gold

Buttoned-Up Ornaments
Heart
Cut 1 red

Continued on page 31

MELT-YOUR-HEART SNOWMEN ORNAMENTS

By Julie DeGroat

Bundled up to their frosty little noses, these cool, snowy-white guys are sweethearts!

Project Specifications
Skill Level: Beginner
Ornament Size: Approximately 2½" x 5½"

Materials
Note: Materials and instructions are for a set of three snowmen.

- White felt 5" x 16"
- Scraps of red, gold and blue felt
- 8 (½" –¾") craft buttons
- Polyester fiberfill
- 6 black seed beads for eyes
- 6-strand embroidery floss to match or contrast with felt
- Basic sewing supplies and tools

Instructions
Step 1. Trace and cut felt as directed on patterns.
Step 2. With 2 strands of embroidery floss in color of

your choice, work buttonhole or running stitch around two layers of snowman body. Start at head and go around body to within 1" of starting point. Stuff with polyester fiberfill and finish sewing to starting spot.

Step 3. With 2 strands of embroidery floss in color of your choice, work buttonhole or running stitch around two layers of each hat. Start at brim, sew around top of hat and back to other brim, leaving bottom of hat open. Do not fasten off thread. Insert snowman's head into hat and sew with a deliberately long running stitch across base of hat and through head.

Step 4. Position matching scarf on each snowman's front. Place scarf back behind snowman's neck, matching ends to scarf front. With a deliberately long running stitch, sew across all layers—scarf front, snowman and scarf back.

Step 5. Sew seed beads in place for eyes. Referring to photo, trim with craft buttons, sewing onto hat, scarf or body. ✻

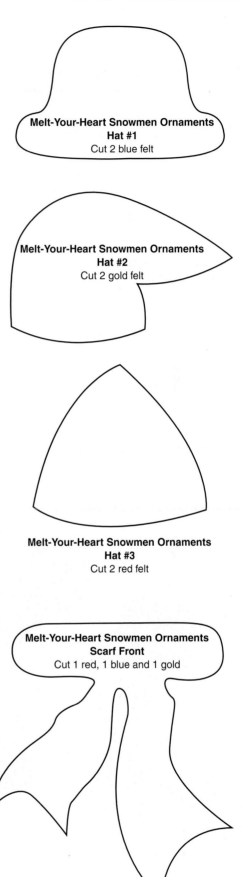

Melt-Your-Heart Snowmen Ornaments
Hat #1
Cut 2 blue felt

Melt-Your-Heart Snowmen Ornaments
Hat #2
Cut 2 gold felt

Melt-Your-Heart Snowmen Ornaments
Hat #3
Cut 2 red felt

Melt-Your-Heart Snowmen Ornaments
Scarf Front
Cut 1 red, 1 blue and 1 gold

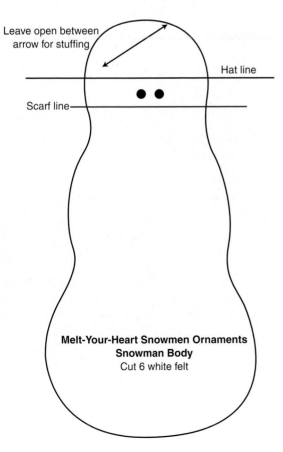

Melt-Your-Heart Snowmen Ornaments
Scarf Back
Cut 1 red, 1 blue and 1 gold

Leave open between arrow for stuffing

Hat line

Scarf line

Melt-Your-Heart Snowmen Ornaments
Snowman Body
Cut 6 white felt

STAR BABY BEANBAGS

By Connie Matricardi

You're the designer of expressions and clothing for these cute babies. Have fun personalizing them for recipients!

Project Specifications
Skill Level: Beginner
Star Baby Size: Approximately 6½" x 7½"

Materials
- Two 9 " x 12" rectangles each of peach, light blue and purple felt
- Craft pellets for stuffing
- All-purpose threads to match felt
- Polyester fiberfill
- Light blue, black, lavender, peach, gray, pink, terra-cotta, white and light yellow acrylic paint
- Artist's brushes of various sizes

- Fine-tip permanent black marker
- Air-soluble marker
- White marking pencil
- Basic sewing supplies and tools

Instructions
Note: When painting on felt, use a light touch. It will be necessary to dab on extra paint to fill in solid areas. A second coat will be necessary when using light-colored paint on dark-colored felt.

Step 1. Trace and cut star babies as directed on pattern.

Step 2. Sew two matching star baby shapes together using ¼" seam allowance. Leave a 2¼" opening at one side for turning and stuffing. Turn right side out.

Step 3. Using face pattern, trace face on each star baby. Use air-soluble marker for light felt colors and white marking pencil for dark.

Step 4. For peach star baby, using photo as a guide, paint face with

terra-cotta acrylic paint. When paint is dry draw eyes and mouth with air-soluble marker, then trace with permanent black marker. Paint a white ⅜" border around face to represent snowsuit hood. Using air-soluble marker draw a simple zipper shape on body. Paint with gray. When paint is dry use permanent black marker to draw small lines as zipper detail. Make polka dots on body with lavender paint.

Step 5. For light blue star baby, using photo as a guide, paint face as in Step 4, using peach paint. Use air soluble marker to draw a ½"-wide scarf around neck. Paint entire scarf white. When

paint is dry, paint stripes with lavender. Paint three small black buttons.

Step 6. For purple star baby, using photo as a guide, paint face as in Step 4, using peach paint. With white marking pencil draw three strands of hair and down center front draw a circle, heart and star. Paint hair yellow, circle white, heart pink and star blue. When white circle is dry, squiggle with lavender.

Step 7. Stuff star baby heads lightly with polyester fiberfill. Fill legs and approximately ⅔ of body with craft pellets. Using small, tight stitches, sew opening closed by hand. ❦

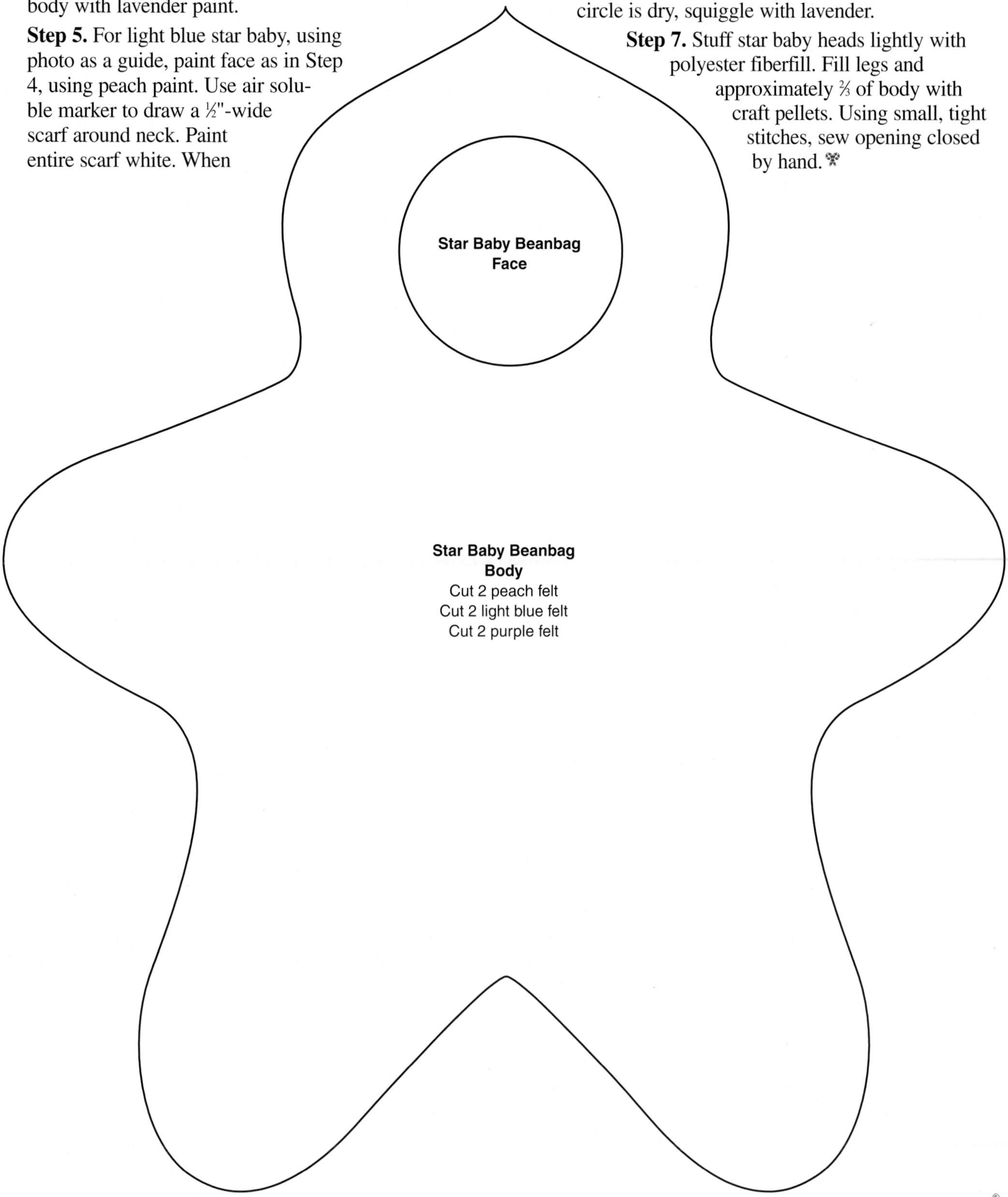

Star Baby Beanbag Face

Star Baby Beanbag Body
Cut 2 peach felt
Cut 2 light blue felt
Cut 2 purple felt

LOG CABIN ANGELS

By Norma Storm

This threesome of country angels will bless your home from the boughs of your Christmas tree.

Project Specifications
Skill Level: Beginner
Angel Size: Approximately 3" x 5"

Materials
Note: Materials and instructions are for one angel.

- Light and dark fabric scraps
- Tiny yellow scrap
- White felt 7" x 7"
- Red or blue felt 3" x 3"
- Polyester fiberfill
- 10" (⅛"-wide) cream satin ribbon for hanger
- 10" (⅛"-wide) coordinating satin ribbon for bow
- All-purpose threads to match fabrics
- Red-and-white-striped pipe cleaner
- Craft glue
- Rotary-cutting tools
- Sharp scissors
- Basic sewing supplies and tools

Instructions
Step 1. Sort fabric scraps into lights and darks. Press and cut into 1"-wide strips. Starting with a 1" x 1" light square and a 1" x 1" dark square make a Log Cabin block adding light and dark logs as shown in Figure 1. Repeat for two squares 4" x 4".

Step 2. Trace and cut heads, wings and mittens as directed on patterns.

Step 3. Place two wings together and stitch ½" from outer edge leaving straight inner edge open. Repeat with other two wing pieces. With sharp scissors clip outer stitched edges of both wings almost to sewing line at ⅛" intervals as shown in Fig. 2.

Step 4. Place two head pieces together. Stitch ½" from outer edge, leaving bottom open. Fringe outer stitched edge of head at ⅛" intervals as in Step 3. Stuff head lightly with polyester fiberfill.

Step 5. Place two mittens together and pin wrist edge to one light side of one Log Cabin block 1" from top edge as shown in Fig. 3. Place light side of second Log Cabin block on top of first. Pin and sew center front seam with mittens in it.

Step 6. Turn up ¼" and sew narrow hem across bottom of the two Log Cabin blocks. Turn under ¼" at top edge of blocks and using hand-basting stitch sew hem. Do not knot ends. Leave threads hanging.

Step 7. Pin one set of wings to each of the back edges as shown in Fig. 3., placing tops of wings ¾" above basted edge. Stitch back seam with wings in it. Turn right side out.

Step 8. Pin head above mittens with neck inside blocks. Pull basting threads tight around neck area and sew by hand to secure head in place. With coordinating ⅛"-wide satin ribbon tie bow around angel's neck.

Step 9. With cream satin ribbon fasten a loop to back of neck for hanging.

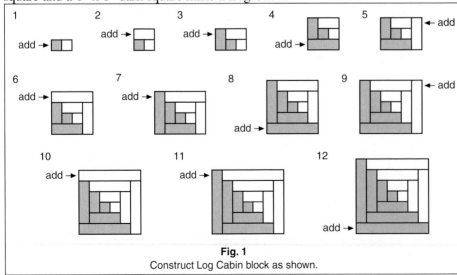

Fig. 1
Construct Log Cabin block as shown.

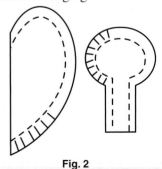

Fig. 2
Clip to seams at ⅛" intervals as shown.

Step 10. Cut 2" length of red-and-white-striped pipe cleaner. Cut candle flame as directed on pattern. Glue one flame to each side of one end of pipe cleaner. Glue or stitch between mittens referring to photo.

Note: For alternate trims cut 3" piece of red-and-white-striped pipe cleaner and bend to form candy cane. Attach as in Step 10. For book trim, cut 1½" x 2" piece of white felt and 1" x 1½" piece of fabric. Place fabric on felt and stitch down center. Fold and glue or stitch to mittens. ❦

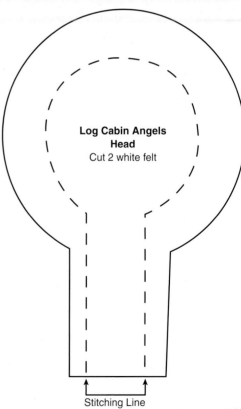

Log Cabin Angels Head
Cut 2 white felt

Stitching Line

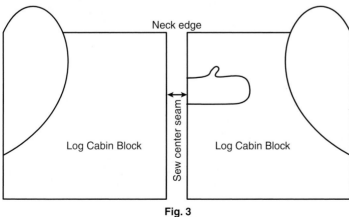

Neck edge

Log Cabin Block

Sew center seam

Log Cabin Block

Fig. 3
Place mittens and wings in seams as shown.

Patterns continued on page 31

CHRISTMAS ELVES SHELF SITTERS

By Connie Matricardi

Not only are these little rascals cute perched on any level surface in your house, they are also very spunky hanging on the tree, doorknobs and handles.

Project Specifications
Skill Level: Beginner
Elf Size: Approximately 3" x 8"

Materials
- Two 9" x 12" pieces each red, green and gold felt
- Scraps of ivory and tan felt
- Scraps of red, green and gold small plaids, prints or stripes
- All-purpose thread to match fabrics
- Polyester fiberfill
- 1 package (4mm) mixed-color round plastic beads
- 9 (10mm) black sequins
- Black 6-strand embroidery floss
- Black pearl cotton floss
- Embroidery needle
- Craft glue
- Air-soluble marker
- Basic sewing supplies and tools

Instructions
Step 1. Trace and cut materials as directed on patterns.

Step 2. From each of three fabric scraps cut three strips 1¾" x 6". Fold raw edges to center lengthwise as shown in Fig. 1; press. Fold in half and press again. Stitch close to the edge. Repeat for three pieces of three fabrics.

Step 3. For arms, cut one strip in half to make two arms. Position arms on contrasting felt body shape as shown in Fig. 2. Pin second body shape of same color to the first and sew front to back, leaving bottom open. Turn right side out.

Step 4. Referring to photo, position three black sequins on body front. Sew to body, attaching a coordinating round plastic bead at the same time using thread to match bead. Repeat for all elf bodies.

Step 5. Stuff body with polyester fiberfill. Referring to photo, position two matching print fabric strips for legs at bottom edge of body. Pin in place. Attach round body base to body using a slip stitch and matching thread.

Step 6. Position one face on each star shape. Sew two black beads to face as eyes. Use air-soluble marker to draw a smiling mouth on each face. Stitch each mouth with two strands of black embroidery floss. Glue completed face and star shape to body.

Step 7. Glue two mittens to each matching fabric arm to enclose ends. Glue two boots to each matching leg to enclose ends.

Step 8. With embroidery needle and 12" piece of black pearl cotton attach a hanging loop to each elf at top of cone. ✾

Fig. 1
Fold edges to center; press.
Fold again and stitch.

Fig. 2
Position arms as shown.

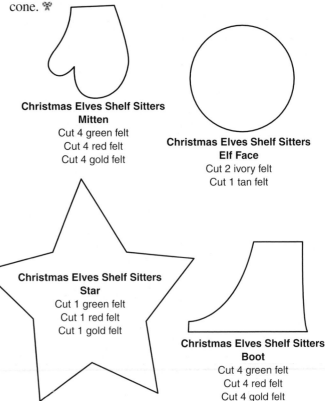

Christmas Elves Shelf Sitters
Mitten
Cut 4 green felt
Cut 4 red felt
Cut 4 gold felt

Christmas Elves Shelf Sitters
Elf Face
Cut 2 ivory felt
Cut 1 tan felt

Christmas Elves Shelf Sitters
Star
Cut 1 green felt
Cut 1 red felt
Cut 1 gold felt

Christmas Elves Shelf Sitters
Boot
Cut 4 green felt
Cut 4 red felt
Cut 4 gold felt

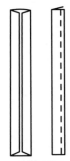

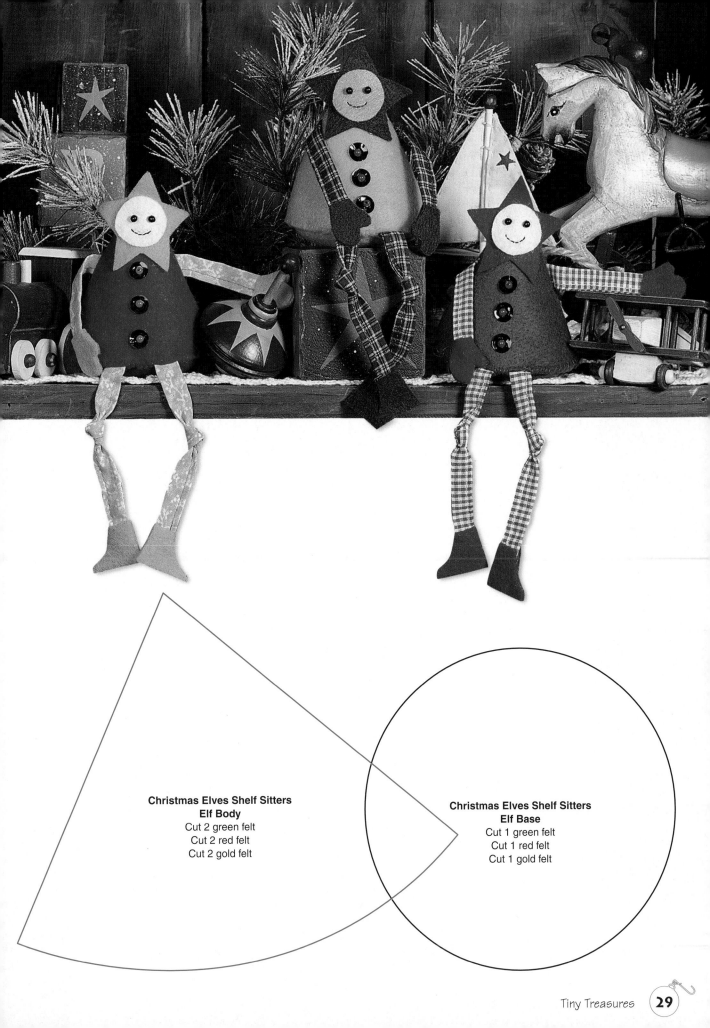

**Christmas Elves Shelf Sitters
Elf Body**
Cut 2 green felt
Cut 2 red felt
Cut 2 gold felt

**Christmas Elves Shelf Sitters
Elf Base**
Cut 1 green felt
Cut 1 red felt
Cut 1 gold felt

Angel Garland

Continued from page 15

ends of garland. Cut 1"-wide green grosgrain ribbon in half and tie each piece to remaining two wreaths with an overhand knot. Trim ribbon ends in a V-cut.

Step 10. To assemble, place angels in an alternating pattern, starting and ending with a red angel. Insert a wreath with a vine bow between each angel and glue hands over side edges of wreath. Glue wreath with ribbon knot to hand of end angels with ribbon on side opposite hand. 🎋

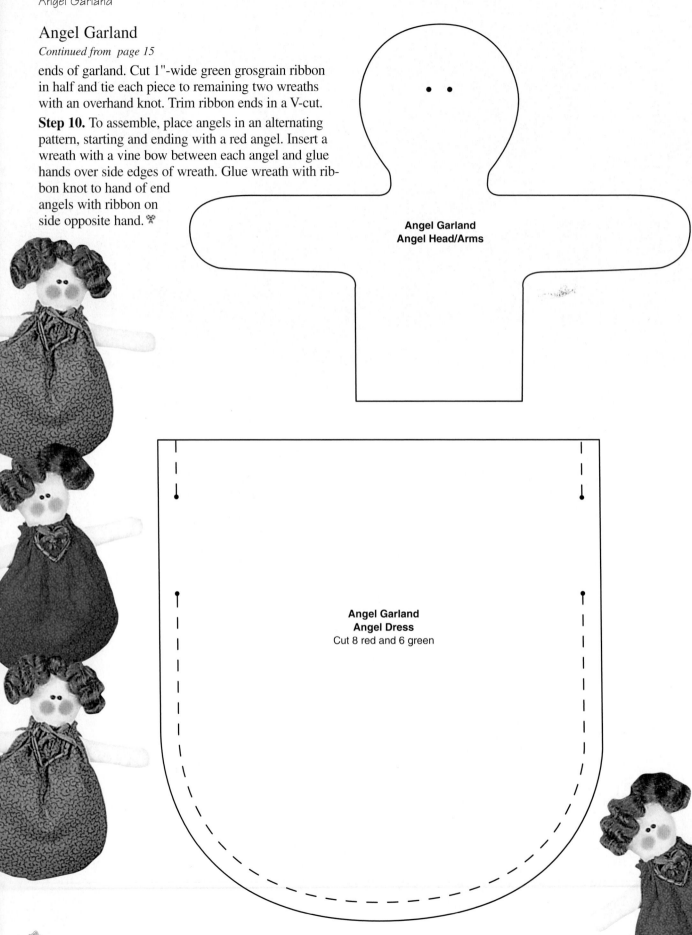

**Angel Garland
Angel Head/Arms**

**Angel Garland
Angel Dress**
Cut 8 red and 6 green

Hallelujah Angel Pin

Continued from page 20

Step 6. Place body front and back together, right sides facing. Stitch all around leaving a 1½" opening at bottom of skirt for turning. Clip curves and turn. Finger-press turned seam.

Step 7. Stuff angel lightly with polyester fiberfill. Turn up skirt opening and close, using one strand of green embroidery floss and a blind stitch.

Step 8. Bundle three tiny twigs and glue in place just below neckline on back of angel. Cut a 1" x 1" square of green fabric and glue over this attachment area. Glue jewelry pin closure to back and let dry.

Step 9. Using cotton-tip swab and powdered blush highlight cheeks. Spray a fine mist of clear acrylic sealer to face. ❀

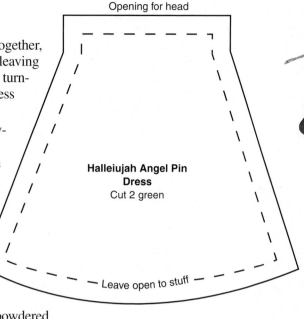

Opening for head

Halleiujah Angel Pin Dress
Cut 2 green

Leave open to stuff

Hallelujah Angel Pin Head
Cut 2 linen or muslin

Buttoned-Up Ornaments

Continued from page 21

HEART

Step 1. Cut two 3" circles from purple wool or felt. Trace and cut heart as directed on pattern and pin to one purple circle.

Step 2. Repeat Star Steps 2–4 for appliqué and finishing.

TREE

Step 1. Cut two 3" circles from teal wool or felt. Trace and cut tree and tree trunk as directed on pattern and pin to one teal circle.

Step 2. Repeat Star Steps 2–4 for appliqué and finishing. ❀

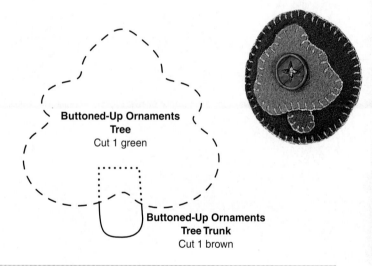

Buttoned-Up Ornaments Tree
Cut 1 green

Buttoned-Up Ornaments Tree Trunk
Cut 1 brown

Log Cabin Angels

Continued from page 27

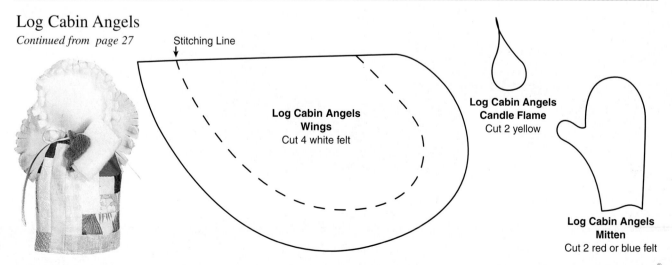

Stitching Line

Log Cabin Angels Wings
Cut 4 white felt

Log Cabin Angels Candle Flame
Cut 2 yellow

Log Cabin Angels Mitten
Cut 2 red or blue felt

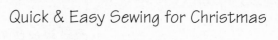

HOLLY JOLLY ACCENTS

Turn your house into a warm Christmas home with the addition of any of these easily sewn decorating accents.

Quick as a wink, you'll finish stockings and tree skirts to keep or give away. We've even included a bone-shaped stocking for your favorite dog pal! And just for cat lovers, add a whimsical touch to your front door with our Santa Kitty Draft Stopper.

Make a holiday decorating statement with one of these projects!

GILDED STARS TREE SKIRT

By June Fiechter

Golden and shiny and very pretty placed under your Christmas tree. Almost too pretty to top with gifts. ...

Project Specifications
Skill Level: Beginner
Tree Skirt Size: Approximately 30" in diameter

Materials
- 2 round pieces of off-white fabric 37" in diameter
- 44" off-white purchased or self-made bias tape
- $\frac{1}{16}$"-wide gold braid
- Gold metallic thread
- All-purpose off-white thread
- Batting circle 37" in diameter
- 3½ yards 1"-wide pleated gold trim
- Basic sewing supplies and tools

Instructions
Step 1. Mark the center of fabric and batting circles and cut a 3" round hole in the center of each. Cut one straight line from center to edge of each circle.

Step 2. Trace whole decorative pattern on center of circle. Trace half of pattern at four sides of circle as shown in Fig. 1.

Step 3. Using zigzag stitch and gold metallic thread attach $\frac{1}{16}$"-wide gold braid to drawn patterns. Do not stitch center circles at this time.

Step 4. Stitch 1"-wide pleated gold trim to right side of decorated fabric circle, facing trim in toward center. Place two fabric circles right sides together and place batting at back of decorated circle. Sew the circles together at outer edge only. Turn right side out and press.

Step 5. Zigzag decorative circles in center of stars, omitting those at opening.

Step 6. Pin-baste top. With off-white thread machine-quilt around each gold braid star. Quilt a wavy line from center star to outer edges of other stars as shown in Fig. 2.

Step 7. Topstitch around outer edge of tree skirt.

Step 8. Bind raw edges of opening to finish. ❧

Pattern continued on page 49

Fig. 1
Trace decorative pattern on skirt
as shown.

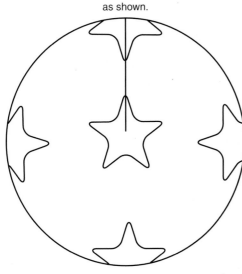

Fig. 2
Machine-quilt lines as shown.

PEEK-A-BOO GIFT BAGS

By Chris Malone

Three different windows of opportunity for showing off your perfectly baked or hand-crafted goodies.

Project Specifications
Skill Level: Beginner
Bag Size: Approximately 6½" x 10" x 2"

Materials
For Each Bag
- 2 pieces of fabric 9" x 12"
- Assorted fabric scraps for appliqué
- Clear vinyl 4½" x 5½"
- 2½" x 30" fabric strip or 1" x 30" ribbon
- 1 (1") button
- Scraps of fusible transfer web
- All-purpose threads to match or contrast with fabrics
- Tape
- Basic sewing supplies and tools

For Tags
- 2¾" x 5" card stock or brown kraft paper
- 6" piece pearl cotton or cord
- Hole punch

Optional Trim for Tree Bag and Tag
- Gold and red acrylic paint
- Paintbrush
- Black fine-line permanent marker
- Fabri-Tac Permanent Adhesive from Beacon
- 1 (⅞") wooden star
- 1 (1¼") wooden star
- 3 (¾") wooden circles

Instructions
Note: Refer to photo throughout. All seams are ¼".

HEART BAG

Step 1. Draw a 4" x 5" rectangle on paper side of fusible transfer web; cut out about ¼" from lines. Following manufacturer's directions, fuse to wrong side of red appliqué fabric and cut out on lines. Position rectangle on right side of one bag rectangle with bottom of appliqué 3¼" up from bottom of bag; fuse in place.

Step 2. Use pattern to draw heart in center of appliquéd rectangle; cut out on lines through rectangle and bag. Cut a 4" x 5" piece of clear vinyl and place on wrong side of fabric, covering cutout area. Hold in place with small pieces of tape. With matching or contrasting thread, topstitch very close to edges of heart and appliquéd rectangle.

Step 3. Pin bag front and back together, right sides facing, and sew around bag, leaving open at top. To make bag bottom, match bottom seam with adjacent side seams; flatten to form a point. Pin seams together and sew 1" from point, perpendicular to seam, through both layers as shown in Fig. 1. Trim seam allowance to ¼". Repeat for other corner. Turn bag right side out.

Fig. 1
Stitch across corners of bag to make bag bottom.

Step 4. Fold and press a double ⅜" hem at top of bag and sew ¼" from fold.

Step 5. For fabric tie, fold 2½" x 30" strip in half lengthwise, right sides facing, and sew raw edges together leaving a 3" opening on long edge to turn. Clip corners and turn right side out; press. Fold in seam allowance on opening and close with hand stitches.

Step 6. Holding tie (or ribbon) 1¼" from top of bag at center back, sew button through tie and bag back to attach. Bring ends around to front and tie in a bow to finish.

HOUSE BAG

Step 1. Use patterns to draw house, roof and chimney on paper side of fusible transfer web; cut out about ¼" from lines. Fuse to selected fabrics and cut out on lines. Position pieces on right side of one bag rectangle, with bottom of house 2" from bottom of bag, and roof overlapping house and chimney ¼"; fuse.

Step 2. Mark a 3"-wide and 2½"-tall rectangle in center of house; cut out on lines. Cut a 4" x 3½" piece of clear vinyl and place on wrong side of fabric, covering cutout area. Hold in place with small pieces of tape. With matching or contrasting thread, topstitch around house, roof, chimney and opening.

Step 3. Finish bag in same manner as Heart Bag, Steps 3–6.

TREE BAG

Step 1. Draw a 4½" x 5½" rectangle on fusible web and fuse to bag as in Heart Bag, Step 1. Position 2" up from bottom.

Step 2. Use pattern to draw tree in center of appliquéd rectangle. Repeat Heart Bag, Step 2, cutting clear vinyl 4½" x 5½". Topstitch around tree and rectangle.

Step 3. Finish bag as in Heart Bag, Steps 3–6.

Step 4. Paint large star gold and circles red. Use black fine-line permanent marker to draw short stitch lines around edges of wooden pieces. Glue star to top of tree and circles to vinyl tree opening.

TAGS

Step 1. Use patterns to draw appropriate appliqués on paper side of fusible transfer web. Cut out just outside lines and fuse to selected fabrics. Cut out on lines.

Step 2. Fold card stock or brown paper in half crosswise. Fuse appliqués to tag.

Step 3. Punch hole in top left corner of card. Thread pearl cotton through hole; tie ends in a knot and trim close to knot. Slip over one bag tie before closing bag.

Step 4. For tree tag only, paint and glue small star to top of tree. ❦

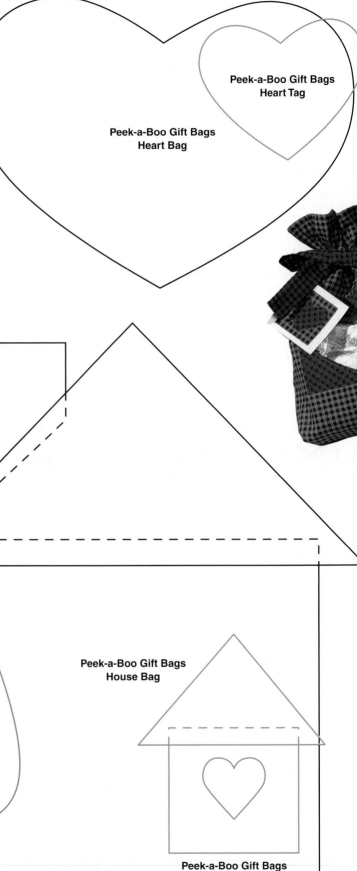

**Peek-a-Boo Gift Bags
Heart Bag**

**Peek-a-Boo Gift Bags
Heart Tag**

**Peek-a-Boo Gift Bags
House Bag**

**Peek-a-Boo Gift Bags
House Tag**

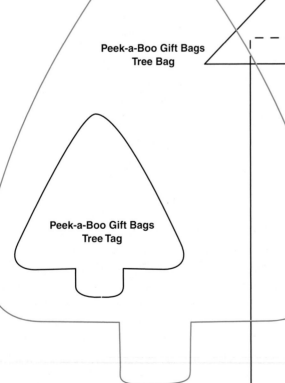

**Peek-a-Boo Gift Bags
Tree Bag**

**Peek-a-Boo Gift Bags
Tree Tag**

THE HEART OF CHRISTMAS

By Barbara E. Swanson

Three ways to go with one pattern. Which will you choose? Maybe all three?

Project Specifications

Skill Level: Beginner

Large Stocking Size: Approximately 14" x 10"

Small Stocking Size: Approximately 8½" x 6"

Ornament Size: Approximately 4" x 5"

Materials

For 14" Stocking

- ½ yard unbleached muslin
- 2 thin batting scraps 11" x 16"
- ¼ yard red print
- 1 yard ¼" cord
- 1 (½") white button

For 8½" Stocking

- Unbleached muslin 10" x 32"
- 2 thin batting scraps 8" x 10"
- ¼ yard red print
- ⅔ yard ¼" cord
- 1 (⅜") white button

For Ornament

- Red print scraps
- 1 (⅜") white button

For All Patterns

- Green print and yellow print scraps
- Black pearl cotton
- Antique gold 6-strand embroidery floss
- Polyester fiberfill
- Zipper/cording foot for sewing machine
- Scraps of fusible transfer web
- Basic sewing supplies and tools

Instructions

LARGE STOCKING

Step 1. Trace one rectangle 1½" x 2" and enlarged tree pattern on paper side of fusible web. Cut around shapes leaving roughly ½" margin. Fuse tree to green print and rectangle to yellow print following manufacturer's directions.

Step 2. Cut and piece 1½"-wide bias strips of red print to measure 1 yard. Using zipper foot on machine, cover cord with bias strip.

Step 3. Cut two red print hearts from enlarged pattern. Cut ½" slit in center of one heart. With right sides facing, stitch all around heart. Trim and clip seam. Turn right side out and stuff lightly with polyester fiberfill. Close opening with hand stitches.

Step 4. Referring to photo for placement, position tree and patch on stocking front; fuse. With black pearl cotton, accent patch with large straight stitches.

Step 5. Place stocking front right side up on one piece of batting; pin. Baste stocking to batting. Trim away excess batting. Repeat for stocking back. Topstitch around tree shape.

Step 6. Baste piping made in Step 2 along sides and lower edges of stocking front, easing along curves.

Step 7. Stitch heart appliqué to tree. With gold embroidery floss, tie button to heart with a bow. Trim ends.

Step 8. Right sides facing, pin stocking front and back together. Stitch around edges, leaving top open. Trim and clip seam. Turn right side out.

Step 9. From red print, cut hanging loop 5" x 1½". Press under ¼" seam allowance on long edges. Press in half lengthwise, wrong sides facing, and edge-stitch. Bring ends together forming a loop. Baste ends to upper right edge of stocking, loop facing down.

Step 10. With right sides facing, pin lining pieces together. Stitch, leaving top open as well as portion of seam indicated on pattern. Trim and clip seam.

Step 11. With right sides facing, pin stocking and lining together at top edge; stitch. Turn lining right side out and close opening with hand stitches. Insert lining in stocking. Edge-stitch along top of stocking.

SMALL STOCKING

Step 1. Trace one rectangle 1" x 1⅜" and tree pattern on fusible web as in Step 1, Large Stocking, and fuse.

Step 2. Cut and piece 1½"-wide bias strips to measure ⅔ yard. Follow Steps 2–11 above, except cut two red print hearts from same-size heart pattern.

ORNAMENT

Step 1. Trace one rectangle 1" x 1⅜" on fusible-web scrap. Cut out leaving ½" margin around lines. Fuse to yellow print scrap and cut out on lines.

Step 2. From green print, cut two trees, adding ¼" seam allowance. Fuse yellow patch to one tree shape. With black pearl cotton, accent patch with large straight stitches.

Step 3. From red print, cut two red hearts. Prepare as in Large Stocking, Step 3. Stitch to tree as in Step 7.

Step 4. Right sides facing, stitch tree front to tree back leaving opening at bottom for turning. Trim and clip seams.

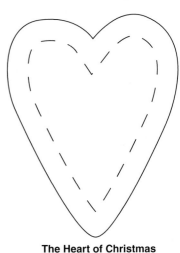

**The Heart of Christmas
Heart**
Cut 2 red print for small stocking
Cut 2 red print for ornament

For Large Stocking Enlarge 137%
Cut 2 red print

Grain line

**The Heart of Christmas
Tree**
Cut 1 green for small stocking
Cut 2 green for ornament
Add ¼" seam allowance

For Large Stocking Enlarge 178%
Cut 1 green

Turn right side out and stuff lightly with polyester fiberfill. Close opening with hand stitches.

Step 5. Stitch hanging loop of gold metallic thread to top of tree. Secure ends with overhand knot and trim. ✳

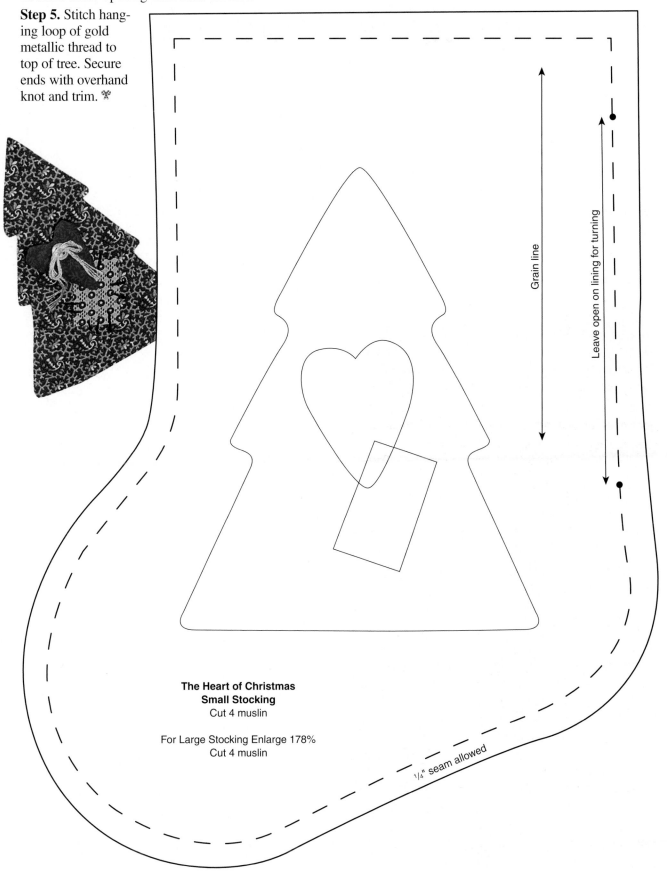

Grain line

Leave open on lining for turning

**The Heart of Christmas
Small Stocking**
Cut 4 muslin

For Large Stocking Enlarge 178%
Cut 4 muslin

1/4" seam allowed

DOGGIE TREATS STOCKING

By Marian Shenk

It's Christmas! Every creature needs a special treat—so give your doggie his own bone stocking!

Project Specifications

Skill Level: Beginner

Stocking Size: Approximately 9" x 14"

Materials

- ⅓ yard green velour or fleece

- ⅓ yard red-and-green plaid
- Scrap of gold fabric for letters
- Off-white metallic print scrap for heart
- 2 (⅝") gold jingle bells
- ½ yard gold metallic braid
- All-purpose threads to match fabrics
- Gold metallic thread
- Scraps of fusible transfer web
- ½ yard ⅜"-wide red ribbon
- 2 thin batting scraps 10" x 16"
- Basic sewing supplies and tools

Instructions

Step 1. Cut patterns, fabrics and batting as directed on templates.

Step 2. Machine-appliqué cuffs to stocking front and back. Machine-appliqué heart to stocking front. Stitch gold metallic braid around edges of heart.

Step 3. Mark a 1" quilting grid on stocking front and back as shown in Figure 1.

Fig. 1
Mark 1" quilting grid on stocking front and back as shown.

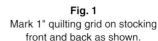

Step 4. Baste one batting piece to back and one to front of stocking. With gold metallic thread, machine-quilt on marked grid.

Step 5. Right sides together, sew stocking front to back, starting and stopping at pattern notches on cuff.

Step 6. Right sides together, sew plaid lining pieces together, also starting and stopping at cuff notches. Slip stocking into lining, right sides together.

Step 7. Cut a piece of stocking fabric 1" x 8". Fold in half lengthwise and stitch along long edge. Turn right side out. Fold in half matching short ends for loop hanger. Insert loop at top corner and sew across raw edges at stocking top.

Step 8. Pull stocking out and push lining inside stocking; press. Close opening with hand stitches.

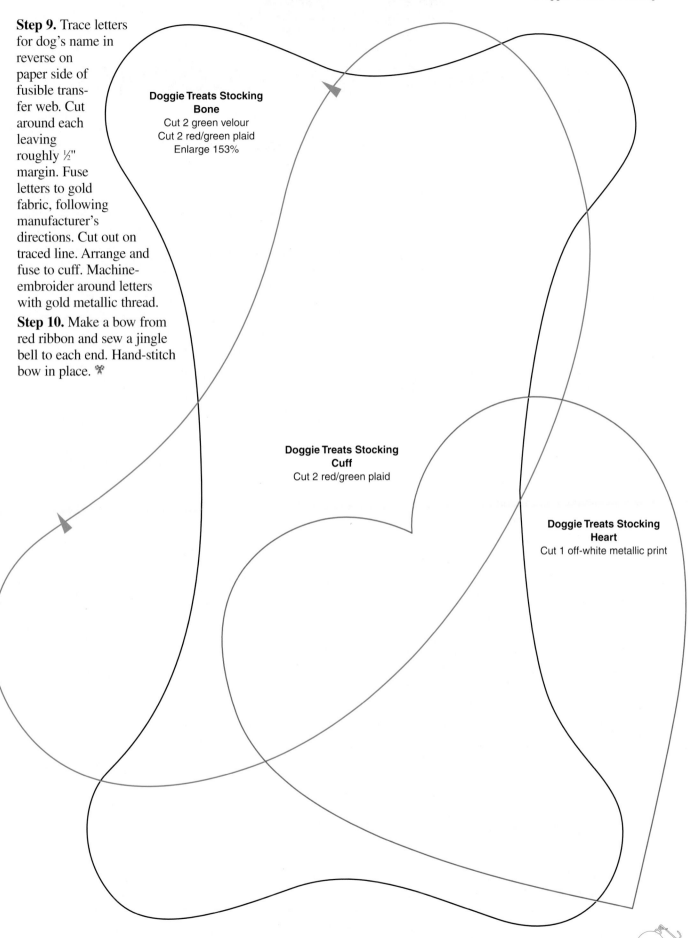

Step 9. Trace letters for dog's name in reverse on paper side of fusible transfer web. Cut around each leaving roughly ½" margin. Fuse letters to gold fabric, following manufacturer's directions. Cut out on traced line. Arrange and fuse to cuff. Machine-embroider around letters with gold metallic thread.

Step 10. Make a bow from red ribbon and sew a jingle bell to each end. Hand-stitch bow in place. ✼

**Doggie Treats Stocking
Bone**
Cut 2 green velour
Cut 2 red/green plaid
Enlarge 153%

**Doggie Treats Stocking
Cuff**
Cut 2 red/green plaid

**Doggie Treats Stocking
Heart**
Cut 1 off-white metallic print

CHRISTMAS TOPIARY STOCKING

By Connie Matricardi

Felt is such an easy material to work with and produces wonderful results with a minimum of fuss and finishing. Enjoy the process as well as the product!

Project Specifications
Skill Level: Beginner
Stocking Size: Approximately 17" x 11"

Materials
- ½ yard antique white felt
- 9" x 12" rectangles of green, red and gold felt
- ½ yard off-white cotton or cotton blend for lining
- Red and green all-purpose thread
- 13" piece of ⅝"-wide red grosgrain ribbon
- Green 6-strand embroidery floss
- 1 (1") gold shank-style star button
- 5 (⅝") gold shank-style star buttons
- 1 package gold 8mm sequins
- 1 package of clear rocaille beads
- Craft glue
- Air-soluble marker
- Basic sewing supplies and tools

Instructions
Step 1. Trace and cut paper patterns. Cut fabric and felt as directed on patterns.

Step 2. Using photo as a guide, position large and small heel and toe pieces and pin. Position and pin tree, trunk, flower pot and birds to stocking front. Glue trunk in place. Tree and pot will overlap trunk. Glue bird bodies and wings in place. When glue is dry, sew a rocaille bead to each bird as an eye.

Step 3. Sew heel and toe pieces, tree and pot to stocking front with matching all-purpose threads.

Step 4. Referring to photo for placement, arrange sequins on stocking. Mark positions with air-soluble marker; remove sequins and sew on one at a time using a rocaille bead for each sequin. Sew four sequins each to pot and stocking toe and heel. Sew five sequins in a line parallel to felt toe piece. Sew large star button to top of tree and five smaller buttons to tree. Sew eight sequins to tree.

Step 5. With air-soluble marker, draw a curved line from tree top to each bird. With 3 strands of green embroidery floss sew a running stitch along each line.

Step 6. Referring to photo, sew five sequins and beads to each red scallop as shown. Position one red scallop on each gold scallop and pin to stocking front. Sew in place across top of stocking with red all-purpose thread.

Step 7. Right sides together, sew lining front and back together, leaving top edge open. Do not turn right side out. Press under ½" at top edge to wrong side.

Step 8. With green thread, wrong sides together, sew stocking front to stocking back leaving top open. Place lining inside stocking, matching seams; slipstitch in place along top edge of stocking.

Step 9. Fold red grosgrain ribbon in half and sew raw edges inside upper corner of stocking. ❦

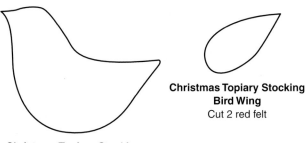

**Christmas Topiary Stocking
Bird Wing**
Cut 2 red felt

**Christmas Topiary Stocking
Bird**
Cut 2 red felt

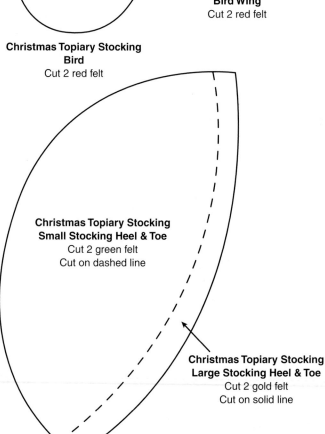

**Christmas Topiary Stocking
Small Stocking Heel & Toe**
Cut 2 green felt
Cut on dashed line

**Christmas Topiary Stocking
Large Stocking Heel & Toe**
Cut 2 gold felt
Cut on solid line

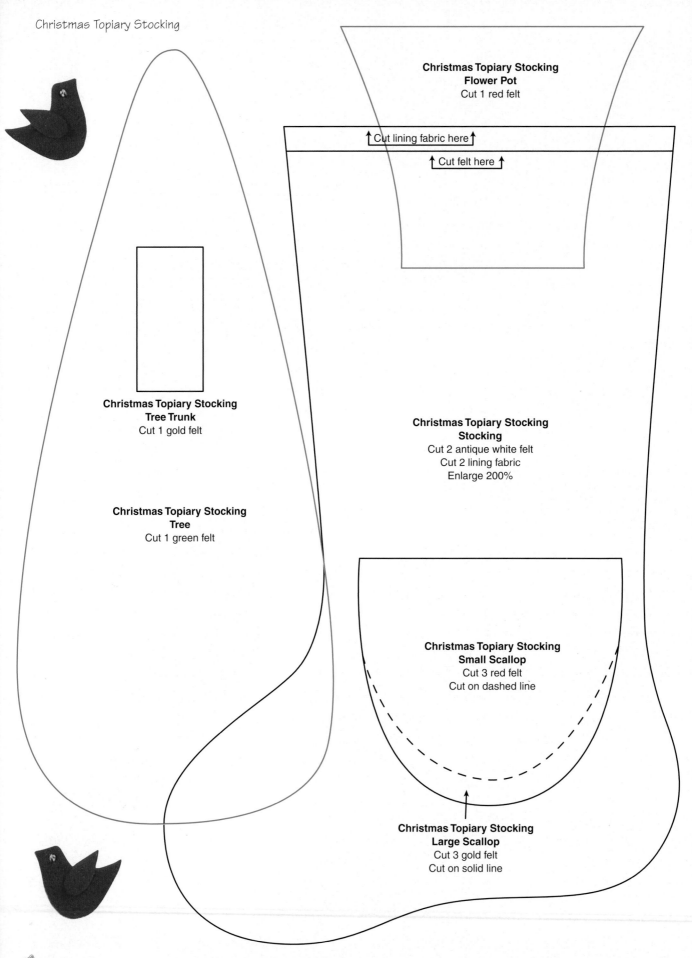

**Christmas Topiary Stocking
Flower Pot**
Cut 1 red felt

↑ Cut lining fabric here ↑

↑ Cut felt here ↑

**Christmas Topiary Stocking
Tree Trunk**
Cut 1 gold felt

**Christmas Topiary Stocking
Tree**
Cut 1 green felt

**Christmas Topiary Stocking
Stocking**
Cut 2 antique white felt
Cut 2 lining fabric
Enlarge 200%

**Christmas Topiary Stocking
Small Scallop**
Cut 3 red felt
Cut on dashed line

**Christmas Topiary Stocking
Large Scallop**
Cut 3 gold felt
Cut on solid line

ELEGANT TASSELED MANTEL SCARF

By Phyllis M. Dobbs

Very rich, very Victorian and a perfectly beautiful way to dress up your mantel for holiday entertaining.

Project Specifications
Skill Level: Beginner
Mantel Scarf Size: Approximately 43" x 10" x 14"

Materials
- ¾ yard green velvet
- ½ yard red velvet
- ¾ yard green lining fabric
- ½ yard red lining fabric
- 3 (3") gold metallic tassels
- 96" gold twisted braid
- Basic sewing supplies and tools

Instructions
Step 1. Cut triangles as directed on patterns. Right sides together, pin each triangle to matching lining piece.

Step 2. Insert tassel at each triangle point. Catch top of tassel in seam line. Pin in place with bottom of tassel pointing away from triangle point.

Step 3. Sew velvet to lining with ¼" seam allowance. Do not stitch along top edge. Trim points, turn and press.

Step 4. Align triangles side by side as shown in photo, with red triangle in the center and a green triangle on each side. Overlap the red triangle edges over the green triangles 5" on each side. Pin edges together and stitch.

Step 5. From green velvet and green lining fabric cut a scarf top 46" x 11".

Step 6. Place triangles on top of velvet scarf top, right sides together and with top edges of triangles aligned with one long edge of scarf top. Place lining on top of triangles. With triangles sandwiched between scarf and lining, pin edges together and stitch seams. Leave a 5" opening along back edge for turning. Turn and press seams.

Step 7. Close opening with hand stitches. Sew gold braid around edges of triangles. ✬

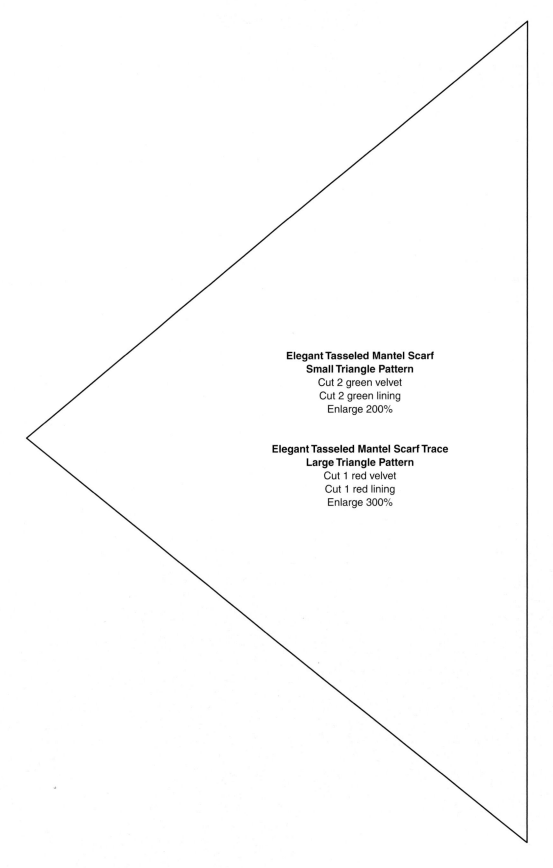

Elegant Tasseled Mantel Scarf
Small Triangle Pattern
Cut 2 green velvet
Cut 2 green lining
Enlarge 200%

Elegant Tasseled Mantel Scarf Trace
Large Triangle Pattern
Cut 1 red velvet
Cut 1 red lining
Enlarge 300%

COUNTRY ANGEL
CHRISTMAS STOCKING

By Phyllis M. Dobbs

This charming stocking is easy enough for children to assemble and finish using fusible appliqué techniques. Let them stuff the stocking with gifts for a teacher or friend.

Project Specifications
Skill Level: Beginner
Stocking Size: Approximately 8" x 15"

Materials
- ⅓ yard natural fabric
- ⅓ yard lining fabric
- Scraps of green, red, blue, tan, gold and brown
- 6 assorted buttons
- 2 star buttons
- 8" piece of ¼"-wide green satin ribbon
- Scraps of fusible transfer web
- Red, green, brown and blue 6-strand embroidery floss
- Embroidery needle
- All-purpose natural thread
- Basic sewing supplies and tools

Instructions
Step 1. Cut stocking and cuff as directed on pattern. Sew together with ¼" seam allowance; press.

Step 2. Trace appliqué shapes on paper side of fusible transfer web as directed. Cut pieces out leaving roughly ½" margin around traced lines.

Step 3. Fuse appliqué shapes to selected fabrics following manufacturer's directions. Referring to photo, arrange on stocking front and fuse.

Step 4. Referring to photo for placement, sew on buttons. With 6 strands of brown embroidery floss, embroider French knots around angel head.

Step 5. Using 3 strands of green embroidery floss, embroider straight stitches around edges of star and stocking heel and toe. With blue embroidery floss, stitch around angel wings. Work a running stitch around tree with red embroidery floss. Stitch a star on each side of angel with long straight stitches and red embroidery floss.

Step 6. Pin stocking front to lining and cut two pieces (reverse 1). Right sides facing, sew two lining

pieces together with ⅜" seam allowance, leaving top edge open.

Step 7. Pin stocking front to fabric for stocking back, wrong sides together. Cut out and stitch together with ¼" seam allowance. Turn right side out; press. Do not turn lining.

Step 8. Fold satin ribbon in half. Pin ends on top of right stocking seam, fold pointing toward bottom of stocking. Match ends to top edge.

Step 9. Place stocking inside lining. Pin top edges together. Stitch with ¼" seam allowance, leaving 2" opening along back edge. Turn right side out and tuck lining into stocking; press. Close opening with hand stitches. ❧

**Country Angel Christmas Stocking
Angel Wing**
Cut 2 red
(reverse 1)

**Country Angel Christmas Stocking
Angel Dress**
Cut 1 blue

**Country Angel Christmas Stocking
Stocking**
Cut 1 natural
Enlarge 154%

**Country Angel Christmas Stocking
Angel Leg**
Cut 2 brown
(reverse 1)

**Country Angel Christmas Stocking
Stocking Cuff**
Cut 1 red & green print
Enlarge 154%

**Country Angel Christmas Stocking
Tree**
Cut 1 green

**Country Angel Christmas Stocking
Star**
Cut 1 gold

Gilded Stars Tree Skirt
Continued from page 34

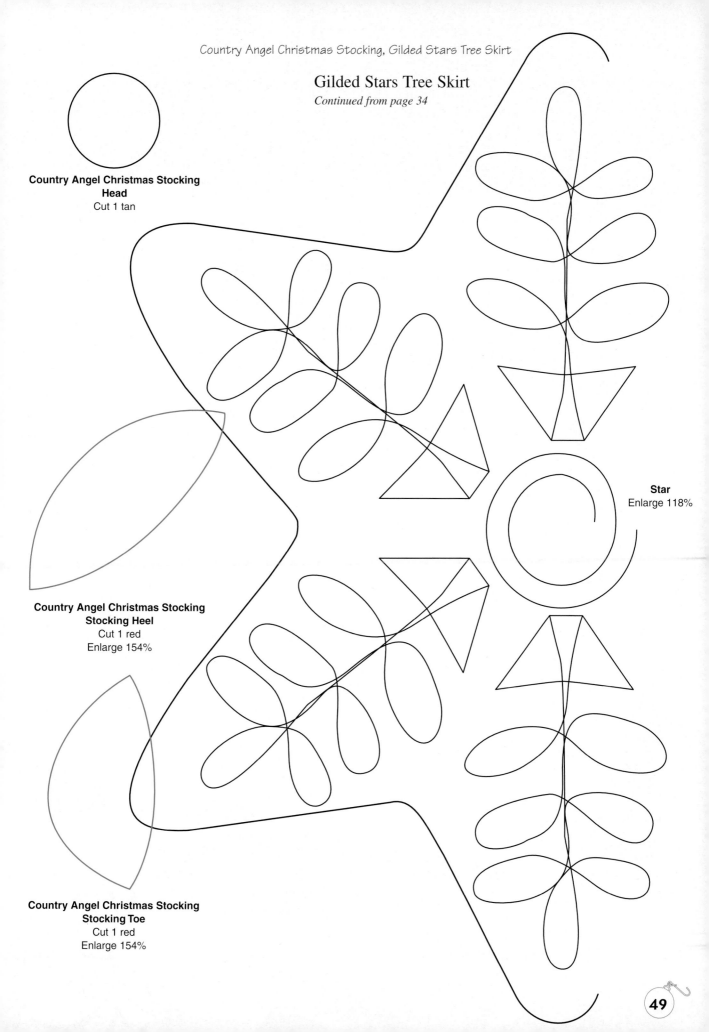

Country Angel Christmas Stocking
Head
Cut 1 tan

Country Angel Christmas Stocking
Stocking Heel
Cut 1 red
Enlarge 154%

Country Angel Christmas Stocking
Stocking Toe
Cut 1 red
Enlarge 154%

Star
Enlarge 118%

CHRISTMAS CARD ENVELOPE

By Kathy Brown

Be prepared for the arrival of Christmas greeting cards. This gold-lined envelope is a great receptacle and is decorative as well.

Project Specifications
Skill Level: Beginner
Envelope Size: Approximately 12" x 16"

Materials
- ½ yard sturdy white fabric
- ½ yard gold satin
- Black, red and green permanent markers
- Disappearing marker
- All-purpose white thread
- Basic sewing supplies and tools

Instructions
Step 1. From sturdy white fabric and gold satin cut one piece each 18" x 38". With right sides together, sew around all sides leaving open where indicated in Fig. 1.

Step 2. Mark a point on the seam line on left side of fabric 12" down from top edge. Draw a 1" horizontal line towards the center of the fabric. Repeat on right side.

Step 3. Mark center point on the top seam line. Draw a diagonal line from top center to each end point on sides as shown in Fig. 2.

Step 4. Stitch on drawn lines. Leaving ¼" seam allowance, cut away excess fabric. Turn right side out through opening; press.

Step 5. White sides together, fold bottom edge up as shown in Fig. 3. Sew a seam down each side. Turn right side out; press.

Step 6. With disappearing marker draw horizontal lines in return and address positions on face of envelope. Write names and addresses as appropriate.

Step 7. Draw 1½" circle for postmark. Enter month and year. Draw wavy lines for postmark cancellation. Trace over all letters and lines with a permanent marker.

Note: Letters and lines can be embroidered by hand or machine if desired. ❄

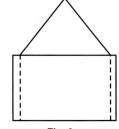

Fig. 3
Fold bottom of envelope up and stitch side seams.

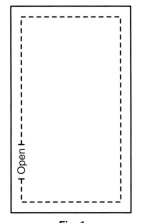

Fig. 1
Stitch around rectangle leaving opening as shown.

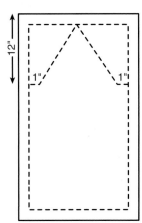

Fig. 2
Mark seam line for flap as shown.

PATCHWORK PETALS TREE SKIRT

By Nancy Brenan Daniel

This is a great project for using many of your favorite Christmas fabric and batting scraps, or purchase eight fabrics for a more coordinated look.

Project Specifications

Skill Level: Beginner

Tree Skirt Size: Approximately 40" x 40"

Materials

- Mixed Christmas fabric scraps totaling 2 yards
- Backing 42" x 42"
- 16 batting pieces 7" x 21"
- All-purpose thread to coordinate with fabrics
- Rotary-cutting tools
- Basic sewing supplies and tools

Instructions

Step 1. From Christmas scraps cut 16 rectangles each 2¾" x 2⅞", 4½" x 5¾" and 6¼" x 5¾". Press or mark a center line on wrong side of each as shown in Fig. 1.

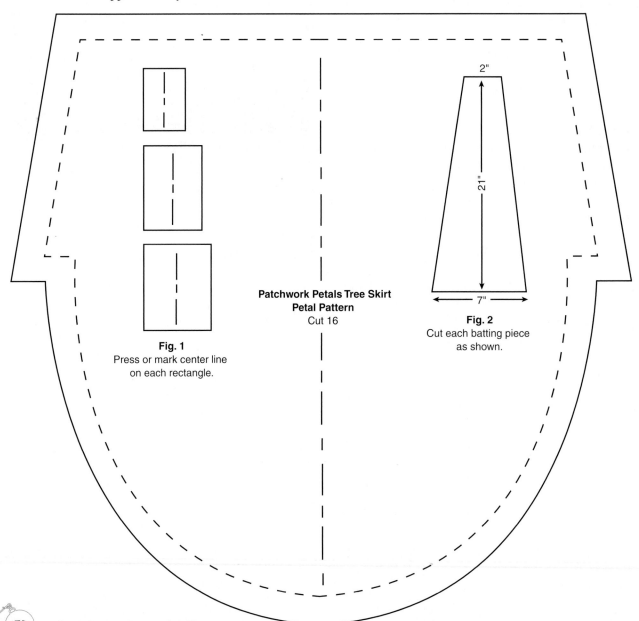

Fig. 1
Press or mark center line
on each rectangle.

Patchwork Petals Tree Skirt
Petal Pattern
Cut 16

2"

21"

7"

Fig. 2
Cut each batting piece
as shown.

Cut petals as directed on pattern.

Step 2. Cut batting in fan shapes as shown in Fig. 2.

Step 3. Place one petal piece wrong side down on lower edge of one batting piece as shown in Fig. 3.

Step 4. Place one rectangle of largest size over petal, right sides together. Match fold lines and align upper fabric edges. Stitch across, flip up and finger-press as shown in Fig. 4. Repeat using mid-size rectangles and again with smallest rectangle. Press completed fan shapes with warm iron (hot may melt batting).

Step 5. On right side of fan measure 1½" across top and mark. Trim fan and batting to this size using template piece at bottom and narrowing to 1½" at top as shown in Fig. 5. Repeat for a total of 16 fan shapes.

Step 6. Sew fan shapes together on long edges leaving opening between first and last. Press seams open or to one side with warm iron.

Step 7. From Christmas scraps cut two strips 4½" x 19" for ties. Fold right sides together and stitch

long edge and across end. Repeat for two ties. Turn right side out; press. Pin one tie to top of each side opening.

Step 8. Place pieced circle over backing square, right sides together. Tuck ties inside away from seam lines. Stitch around all edges with ½" seam allowance. Leave opening on one side for turning. Clip curves and notches along petal edge. Turn right side out through opening. Press with warm iron. Close opening with hand stitches. ✤

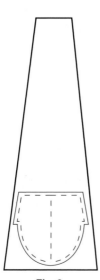

Fig. 3
Place petal piece
on fan as shown.

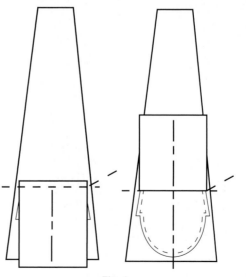

Fig. 4
Align, stitch and flip rectangle as shown.

Fig. 5
Trim as shown.

DAPPER SNOWMAN STOCKING

By Marian Shenk

This stocking is just a bit different in shape and design from most traditional stockings. That makes it a bit more fun, too!

Project Specifications
Skill Level: Beginner
Stocking Size: Approximately 10" x 15"

Materials
- ½ yard white fleece
- ½ yard white cotton for lining
- Black fabric scraps for hat
- Red-and-green plaid scraps
- 2 thin batting scraps 11" x 17"
- ½ yard red wide bias tape for hatband
- 6" black cord for hanging
- All-purpose white thread
- Gold metallic thread
- Black 6-strand embroidery thread
- 1 (1½") gold star button
- Basic sewing supplies and tools

Instructions
Step 1. Cut patterns and fabrics as directed on templates.

Step 2. Machine-stitch hat to stocking front and back.

Step 3. Using stocking front as pattern, cut two linings from white cotton and two from batting.

Step 4. Cut a piece of red-and-white plaid fabric 3½" x 10¼". Right sides together, sew long edges together. Turn right side out; press. Fringe both ends.

Step 5. Place front and back of stocking each on one batting piece. Position toe, heel, hatband and scarf on stocking back and front. Place scarf ends made in Step 4 over and under scarf on stocking front. Appliqué with metallic gold thread and decorative machine stitching.

Step 6. With 2 strands of black embroidery floss, embroider eyes, nose and mouth.

Step 7. Right sides facing, sew stocking front and back together leaving open at top. Turn right side out; press. Right sides facing, sew lining pieces together leaving open at top. Do not turn.

Step 8. Slip stocking into lining, right sides facing. Place ends of black hanging cord at back edge between layers. Loop should point toward bottom of stocking.

Step 9. Stitch around top of stocking. Pull stocking out and stuff lining inside of stocking; press.

Step 10. Stitch gold star to hatband with gold metallic thread. ❦

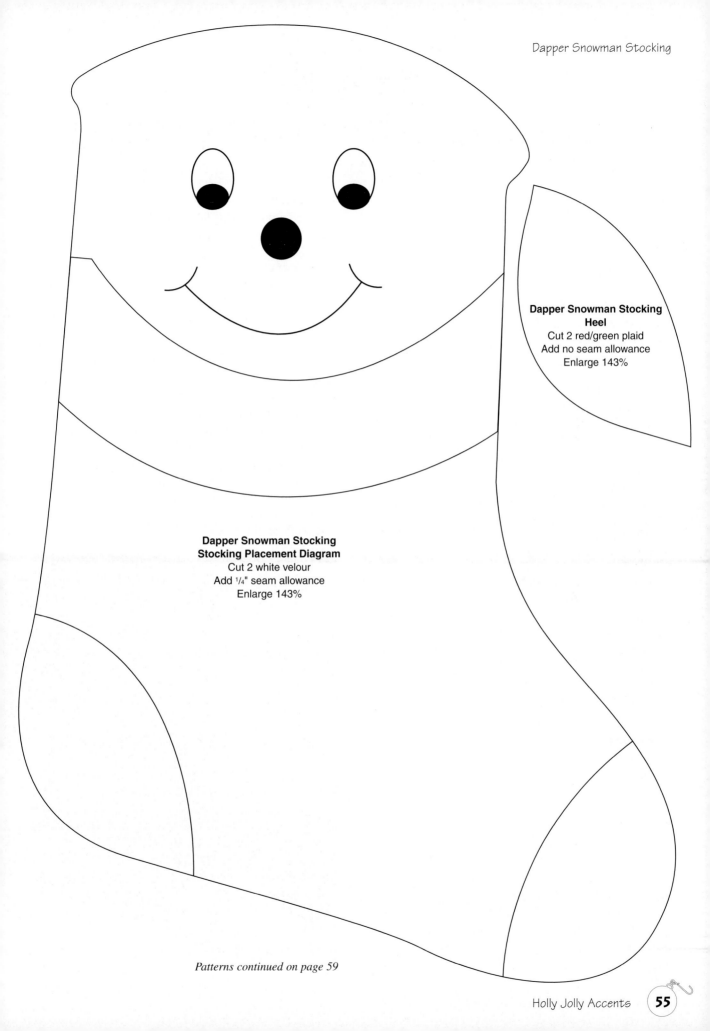

**Dapper Snowman Stocking
Heel**
Cut 2 red/green plaid
Add no seam allowance
Enlarge 143%

**Dapper Snowman Stocking
Stocking Placement Diagram**
Cut 2 white velour
Add ¼" seam allowance
Enlarge 143%

Patterns continued on page 59

CHRISTMAS KITTY DRAFT CATCHER

By June Fiechter

If ever the north wind blows, it's usually at Christmastime. Put this kitty to work so everyone will stay comfy and warm.

Project Specifications

Skill Level: Beginner

Draft Catcher Size: Approximately 44" x 10"

Materials

- ½ yard burgundy fabric
- ¼ yard green fabric
- ½ yard muslin
- Plaid scraps for hatband and mittens
- Blue 12" x 12" triangle for hat
- Blue bias binding to match hat ⅜" x 20"
- ½ yard tan plush felt
- White plush felt 6" circle for face
- Deep rose 1½" felt circle for nose
- White all-purpose thread
- Black 6-strand embroidery floss
- Hot-glue gun and glue
- 60" of 16-guage hardware wire
- Polyester fiberfill
- Scraps of flat batting
- 1" white pompom for hat
- 2 (⅜") round black cabochons for eyes
- Fabric glue
- 6 craft whiskers each 4½" long
- Dried beans or plastic pebble filler
- Basic sewing supplies and tools

Instructions

Note: Refer to photo throughout. Add ½" seam allowance to all pattern pieces.

HEAD

Step 1. Cut a 1¼" circle from batting, hold behind 1½" rose felt nose and position at top of 6" white face circle. Satin-stitch in place with white thread.

Step 2. Cut 2 tan plush felt circles 8" in diameter for head. Cut a 5½" circle from batting. Place on front of one of the head pieces at the bottom. Position white plush felt face on top of batting, nose at top, and satin-stitch in place.

Step 3. Trace pattern and cut ear pieces from tan plush

felt. Sew, right sides together, leaving bottom open. Turn right side out and stuff lightly with polyester fiberfill.

Step 4. Right side up, place second head piece on work surface. Pin ear upside down to top of head piece and place face portion of head right side down on top. Position so ear will be slightly right of nose when finished; pin. Sew around head leaving a 5" opening where second ear will be. Turn right side out and stuff head with polyester fiberfill.

BODY & LEGS

Step 1. From muslin cut two pieces 8" x 18" for legs. Fold each in half lengthwise and sew long edges. Turn right side out. From tan plush felt, trace and cut four feet. Right sides together, sew, turn right side out and stuff with polyester fiberfill.

Step 2. From burgundy fabric cut one piece 7" x 4½" for pants front. Press under a hem on one 7" edge. From tan plush felt cut one piece 7" x 9½" for tummy. Pin pants front to one 7" edge of tummy. Topstitch in place.

Step 3. From burgundy fabric cut two pieces for pants each 8" x 28". Hem one 8"-end of each piece. Fold each in half lengthwise and sew long edges. Turn right side out; press. Pull pants over legs, bunching up pants to fit. Pin raw pants edges to raw leg edges.

Step 4. From muslin cut one piece 8½" x 5½" for body back. Pin raw edges of each leg to front of back edge as shown in Fig. 1, folding legs downward to keep them out of the way.

Step 5. With right sides together, stitch back to tummy, rounding off the shoulders. Leave bottom open. Turn right side out. Stuff shoulder portion firmly with polyester fiberfill. Fill remaining body space with beans or plastic bead filler. Hot-glue bottom edge to close.

Step 6. From ankle end, stuff legs firmly with poly-

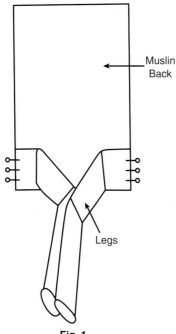

Fig. 1
Pin legs to back as shown.

ester fiberfill. Pull back hems of pants and hot-glue legs to feet, then pull pants back down 1" over foot.

ARMS & JACKET

Step 1. From muslin cut two pieces 8" x 13" for arms. Fold each in half lengthwise and sew long edges and across one short end. Turn right side out and stuff with polyester fiberfill.

Step 2. From green fabric cut two pieces 11" x 8" for sleeves and one piece 9" x 18" for jacket. Mark center of one 8"-edge of each sleeve. Mark center of both 18"-edges of jacket. With right sides together, pin each sleeve to jacket as shown in Fig. 2, matching center marks. Stitch and press seam open. Turn under a hem at each sleeve end and topstitch.

Step 3. Fold jacket right sides together

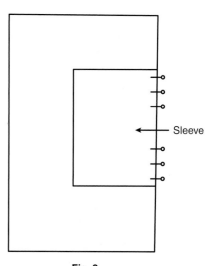

Fig. 2
Match sleeves to jacket
as shown.

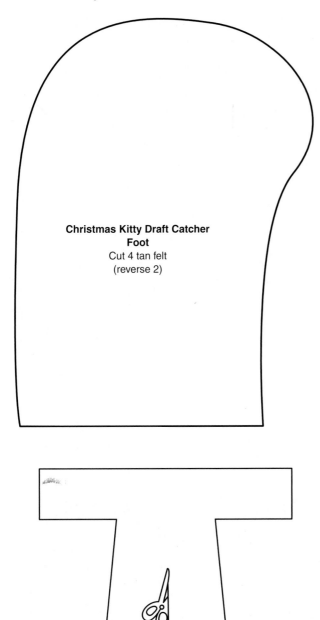

Christmas Kitty Draft Catcher
Foot
Cut 4 tan felt
(reverse 2)

Fig. 3
Slit jacket up front as shown.

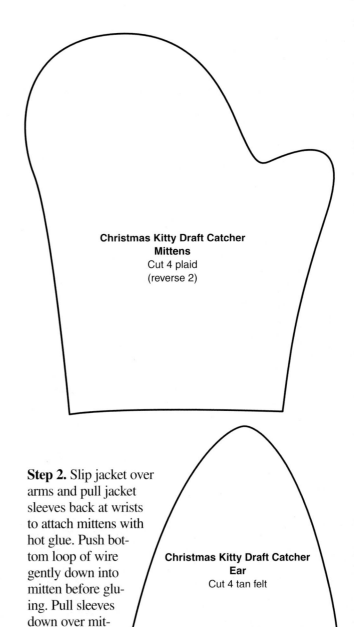

Christmas Kitty Draft Catcher
Mittens
Cut 4 plaid
(reverse 2)

Christmas Kitty Draft Catcher
Ear
Cut 4 tan felt

Step 2. Slip jacket over arms and pull jacket sleeves back at wrists to attach mittens with hot glue. Push bottom loop of wire gently down into mitten before gluing. Pull sleeves down over mitten and hot-glue to secure.

so 9" edges are even. Pin sleeves and jacket sides and sew. Cut slit up jacket front as shown in Fig. 3. Hem bottom of jacket and bind front of jacket with blue bias binding.

MITTENS

Step 1. Trace and cut mittens. Right sides together, stitch fronts to backs, leaving open at wrist. Turn right side out and stuff with polyester fiberfill. Cut hardware wire in half. Bend each piece in half creating a loop at each end. Push one loop into open end of arm to shoulder. Repeat with second arm. Hot-glue shoulder of arm to shoulder area of body.

HAT

Step 1. From plaid fabric cut one 12" x 4" strip for hatband. Right sides together, sew band to one edge of hat triangle. Stitch remaining sides of triangle together to create cone shape. Fold other long edge of hatband under and hot-glue to top of head. Glue white pompom to tip of hat.

FINISHING

Step 1. Hot-glue black cabochons above nose for eyes. Stitch mouth with black embroidery floss. Place whiskers on face and attach each with a dot of fabric glue.

Step 2. Hot-glue head to body. Bend arms into desired position and hot-glue to body, head, and each other at the wrist. ❦

Dapper Snowman Stocking

Continued from page 55

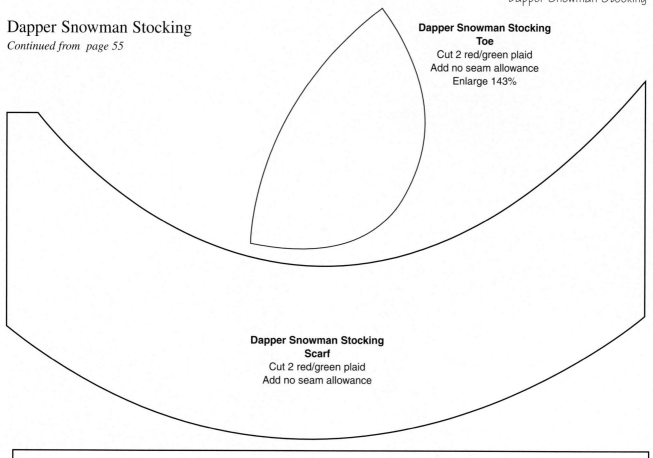

Dapper Snowman Stocking
Toe
Cut 2 red/green plaid
Add no seam allowance
Enlarge 143%

Dapper Snowman Stocking
Scarf
Cut 2 red/green plaid
Add no seam allowance

Dapper Snowman Stocking
Hat
Cut 2 black
Add no seam allowance

FUN & FANCY

C an't figure out what to wear to all those holiday celebrations? Wonder no more!

From tree decorating parties to family dinners, you'll find the perfect wardrobe accent to send you on your way in style. Even the littlest baby will coo and smile as he is admired in his reindeer bib, and his big sister will adore the Christmas outfits you've sewn especially for her.

And because each of these outfits is speedy to create and easy to sew, you can finish one in a hurry for a special last-minute gift!

SNOWY, SNOWY NIGHT SWEATSHIRTS

By June Fiechter

Two different versions of the same theme—both easy, both fast and best of all, warm, snuggly and attractive.

Project Specifications
Skill Level: Beginner
Sweatshirt Size: Any size

Materials
For Zipper Version
- Green sweatshirt in size of your choice
- ¼ yard plaid fabric
- Scrap of gold felt
- White fabric for appliqué
- Blue fabric for appliqué
- ¼ yard fusible transfer web
- 50" black fabric or cord for drawstring
- 5" black zipper
- 1½-yard pieces of red, gold and black yarn
- 4 snowman buttons
- 5 snowflakes

For Collar Version
- Blue sweatshirt in size of your choice
- Scraps of green and white fabric for appliqué
- ¼ yard plaid fabric
- ⅛ yard fusible transfer web
- Scrap of gold felt
- 1½-yard pieces of red, gold and black yarn
- White knit collar
- 3 snowman buttons
- 7 snowflakes

For Both Versions
- Clear nylon monofilament thread
- Fabric glue
- Basic sewing supplies and tools

Note: Launder sweatshirts in cool water with gentle detergent.

Instructions

ZIPPER VERSION
Step 1. Remove cuffs, bottom and neckline ribbing.

Step 2. From plaid fabric cut a facing piece 1¼" x 6".

Right sides together, pin facing to front center of shirt, aligning at neck. Starting at neckline, stitch a U shape wide enough to accommodate zipper. Cut a slit down the U shape through facing and sweatshirt as shown in Fig. 1. Tuck facing through to wrong side of sweatshirt; press. Pin zipper in opening and sew ¼" from edge.

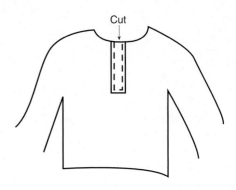

Fig. 1
Cut a slit down the U shape through facing and sweatshirt.

Step 3. From plaid fabric cut 2½"-wide bias strips and join to make 25" piece. Fold in half, wrong sides facing, and press. Apply to neck edge of sweatshirt.

Step 4. From plaid fabric cut two pieces 4" x 14" for cuffs. Right sides together, stitch short ends of cuffs together; press. Pin right side of cuff to inside of sleeve. Stitch and press. Fold back to right side of sleeve, press under raw edge and topstitch to sleeve. Repeat for both sleeves.

Step 5. Find center of lower front edge. Measure up 2" and make a ⅝" buttonhole. Turn under and stitch a 1" hem at bottom edge for casing. Run black drawstring through casing and tie at center front.

Step 6. Trace appliqué shapes on paper side of fusible transfer web as directed on patterns. Cut around shapes roughly ½" outside lines and fuse to selected fabrics. Cut out on traced lines. Referring to photo, arrange on sweatshirt and fuse.

Step 7. Arrange red yarn around plaid shape, and gold yarn around snow, sky and moon. Arrange black yarn between snow and sky. Appliqué yarn and shapes in place with zigzag stitch and clear nylon monofilament.

Step 8. Glue snowmen on snow and snowflakes randomly, referring to photo for ideas.

COLLAR VERSION

Step 1. Cut cuffs and bottom ribbing from sweatshirt. Hem cuffs to desired length.

Step 2. From plaid fabric cut 3"-wide bias strips and join to make enough length to go around bottom of sweatshirt. Fold in half, wrong sides facing, and press. Apply to bottom of sweatshirt.

Step 3. Pin white knit collar to inside of neckband, stretching to fit; stitch.

Step 4. Trace a 4" x 16" rectangle on paper side of fusible web. Trace three squares 3¼" x 3¼". Trace snow shapes and moon as directed on patterns. Cut around each piece leaving ½" margin. Following manufacturer's directions, fuse large rectangle to plaid fabric and small squares to green fabric. Fuse snow shapes to white fabric. Cut on traced lines.

Step 5. Referring to photo, fuse plaid rectangle to sweatshirt front. Fuse snow shapes to green squares and then fuse green squares randomly to sweatshirt. Fuse moon in place.

Step 6. Referring to photo, arrange gold yarn around plaid rectangle and moon. Appliqué yarn and shape in place with zigzag stitch and clear nylon monofilament. Repeat with red yarn around small squares and black yarn along snowline.

Step 7. Glue snowmen and snowflakes in place, referring to photo. ❋

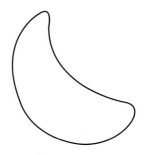

Snowy, Snowy Night Sweatshirts
Collar or Zipper Version
Moon
Cut 1 gold each version

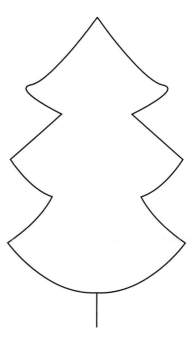

Snowy, Snowy Night Sweatshirts
Zipper Version
Tree
Cut 1 sweatshirt ribbing

Snowy, Snowy Night Sweatshirts
Collar Version
Center Snow Shape
Cut 1 white

Snowy, Snowy Night Sweatshirts
Collar Version
Left Snow Shape
Cut 1 white

Snowy, Snowy Night Sweatshirts
Collar Version
Right Snow Shape
Cut 1 white

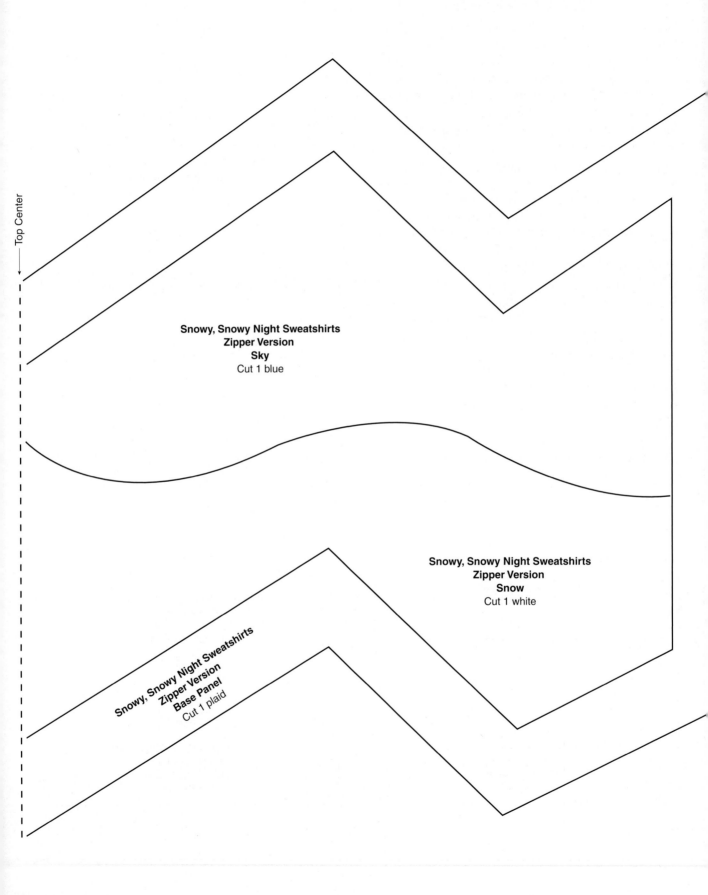

Top Center

Snowy, Snowy Night Sweatshirts
Zipper Version
Sky
Cut 1 blue

Snowy, Snowy Night Sweatshirts
Zipper Version
Snow
Cut 1 white

Snowy, Snowy Night Sweatshirts
Zipper Version
Base Panel
Cut 1 plaid

POINSETTIA COBBLER APRON

By Charlyne Stewart

The cook is probably going to spend a good part of Christmas day in the kitchen. Don't you think she needs a festive cover-up?

Project Specifications
Skill Level: Beginner
Apron Size: Any size

Materials
- Simplicity Pattern 8372
- 2 yards off-white fabric
- ½ yard striped fabric
- Scraps of red and green metallic Christmas prints
- Scraps of gold metallic print
- 4 (¾") white buttons
- ¼ yard fusible transfer web
- Off-white all-purpose thread
- Gold metallic machine-embroidery thread
- Open-toe presser foot
- Basic sewing supplies and tools

Instructions
Step 1. Using commercial pattern fabric layout diagram, pin front and back pieces to off-white fabric. Place a yardstick along side of pattern front and extend line as shown in Fig. 1. Cut out as marked.

Step 2. Cut bias strips from striped fabric as directed on commercial pattern.

Step 3. From off-white fabric cut two pocket pieces 21½" x 8½". Right sides together, stitch around all edges with ¼" seam allowance,

leaving a 3" opening on center bottom. Turn right side out. Turn in seam allowance and hand-stitch to close opening; press.

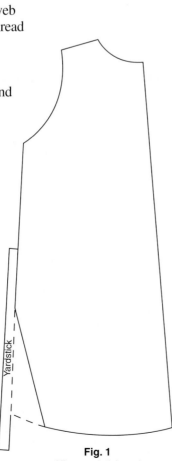

Fig. 1
Align yardstick and extend line as shown.

Step 4. Trace appliqué shapes on paper side of fusible transfer web as directed on patterns. Cut out leaving roughly ½" margin around shapes. Fuse to selected fabrics following manufacturer's directions. Cut out on traced lines.

Step 5. Using photo as a guide, arrange appliqué pieces on left apron front (as worn) and pocket piece; fuse.

Step 6. With medium slightly-open satin stitch, open-toe presser foot and gold metallic thread (off-white in bobbin) outline each piece and interior lines. Repeat using slightly wider stitch setting. Clip loose threads.

Step 7. Pin pocket to apron and topstitch in place. Divide in two or three compartments, if desired.

Step 8. Following commercial pattern directions, sew front and back pieces together. Fold over raw edges of back 1" and press. Fold over 1" again and hem with hand stitches.

Step 9. Apply striped bias binding to neck and armholes. Hem bottom edge.

Step 10. Make four buttonholes 4" apart on back left (as you face it); press. Sew on buttons. ❦

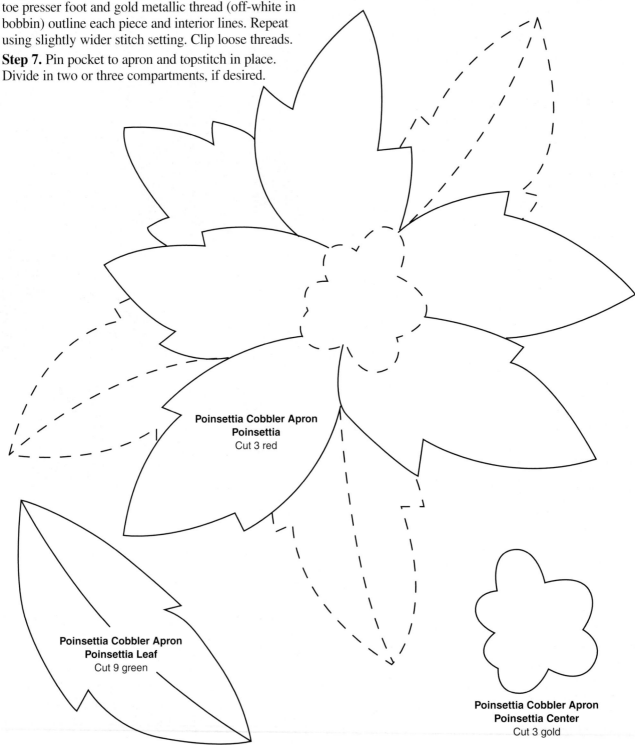

**Poinsettia Cobbler Apron
Poinsettia**
Cut 3 red

**Poinsettia Cobbler Apron
Poinsettia Leaf**
Cut 9 green

**Poinsettia Cobbler Apron
Poinsettia Center**
Cut 3 gold

REINDEER BIB

By Mary Ayres

Baby's adorable Christmas outfit may need a little protection—but provide it in holiday style!

Project Specifications
Skill Level: Beginner
Bib Size: Approximately 8" x 8"

Materials
- ¼ yard light blue print fabric
- ¼ yard light brown solid fabric
- 28" piece white double-fold bias tape
- 1 package bright blue rickrack
- Bright blue 6-strand embroidery floss
- All-purpose white thread
- 1 (⅞") flat red button with 2 holes
- 2 (⅜") flat black buttons with 2 holes
- Firm cotton batting
- Scraps of fusible transfer web
- Basic sewing supplies and tools

Instructions

Step 1. From light blue print fabric cut a 9" x 9" square. Trace bib outline and reindeer antlers on square.

Step 2. Trace reindeer head and ears in one piece on paper side of fusible transfer web. Cut around leaving about ½" margin around traced lines. Fuse, following manufacturer's directions, to light brown solid fabric. Cut out in one piece on traced lines.

Step 3. Position reindeer on bib front; fuse. With 3 strands of bright blue embroidery floss, work buttonhole stitch around reindeer head and ears. Do not embroider lower edge of face, which will be caught in seam. Embroider antlers with stem stitch.

Step 4. Sew black buttons to eye dots with white thread. Angle upper holes of buttons inward.

Step 5. Cut out bib on traced outline. Cut a second bib shape from light blue print for bib back, and another bib shape from batting. Baste batting to

wrong side of bib front. Sew rickrack around bib front (not neckline) ¼" from edge, sewing through center of rickrack.

Step 6. Right sides together, sew bib front to back along rickrack stitching. Turn right side out.

Step 7. Find center of double-fold bias tape and pin to wrong side of center front neckline of bib. Stitch along neckline ¼" from neck edge. Fold tape over to front of bib and pin. Stitch along tape ties and neck edge to close fold.

Step 8. Sew red button at nose dot with white thread, with holes in button running horizontally. ❦

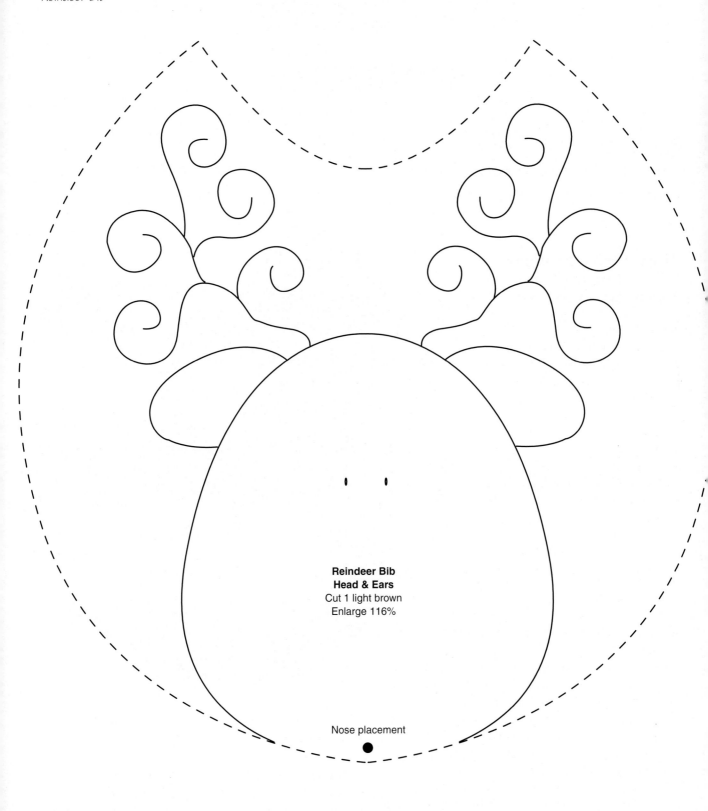

**Reindeer Bib
Head & Ears**
Cut 1 light brown
Enlarge 116%

Nose placement

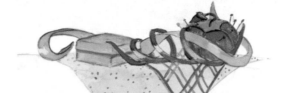

HOLIDAY HOLLY VEST

By Julie Weaver

Pair this holiday top with dressy black pants or skirt for a very elegant evening outfit.

Project Specifications

Skill Level: Beginner

Vest Size: Any size

Materials

- Commercial vest pattern McCalls 2260 or your favorite vest pattern
- Black fabric and lining as required for pattern
- Green/gold metallic fabric scraps for holly leaves
- Red/gold metallic fabric scraps for holly berries
- Scraps of fusible transfer web
- Red, green and gold rayon floss
- All-purpose black thread
- Basic sewing supplies and tools

Instructions

Step 1. Trace appliqué shapes on paper side of fusible transfer web as directed on patterns. Cut out leaving roughly ½" around traced lines. Following manufacturer's directions, fuse to selected fabrics and cut out on traced lines.

Step 2. Arrange appliqué shapes on vest front and back as shown in Fig. 1. Fuse in place.

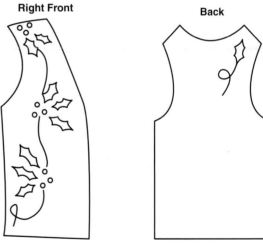

Fig. 1
Arrange appliqué shapes as shown.

Step 3. With 2 strands of red rayon floss work buttonhole stitch around holly berries. With 2 strands of green rayon floss buttonhole-stitch around holly leaves.

Step 4. Referring to Fig. 1, run a light basting stitch between sets of leaves. With 2 strands of gold rayon floss, chain-stitch over basting thread. Remove basting thread.

Step 5. Follow directions on commercial pattern to complete vest construction. ✤

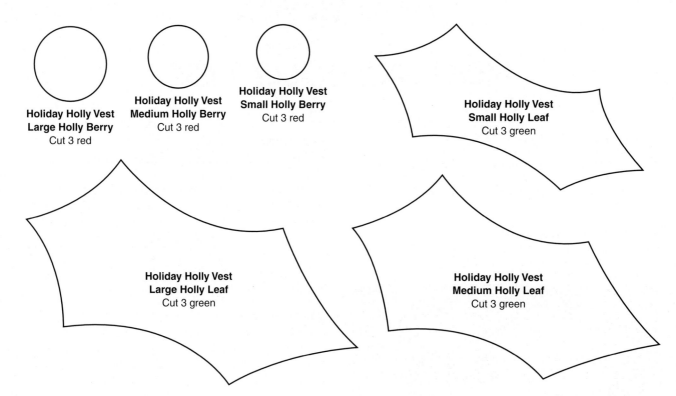

**Holiday Holly Vest
Large Holly Berry**
Cut 3 red

**Holiday Holly Vest
Medium Holly Berry**
Cut 3 red

**Holiday Holly Vest
Small Holly Berry**
Cut 3 red

**Holiday Holly Vest
Small Holly Leaf**
Cut 3 green

**Holiday Holly Vest
Large Holly Leaf**
Cut 3 green

**Holiday Holly Vest
Medium Holly Leaf**
Cut 3 green

TRIO OF TREES DRESS

By June Fiechter

You won't believe how easy this one is—
a T-shirt and a rectangle of soft flannel
and you're on your way!

Project Specifications
Skill Level: Beginner
Dress Size: Any size

Materials
- 2 yards light blue flannel
- Basic navy T-shirt (size 14/16)
- Green-print lightweight cotton scraps for appliqué
- Scraps of fusible transfer web
- Navy and light blue all-purpose threads
- 1 (⅝") star button
- Basic sewing supplies and tools

Instructions
Step 1. Measure down 2½" from armpit of T-shirt and cut off bottom of shirt. From the cut-off portion cut a 6¼" x 5¾" piece for a pocket.

Step 2. Trace appliqué shapes as directed on pattern, and one rectangle 6¼" x 6¾", on paper side of fusible transfer web. Cut out roughly ½" around traced lines. Fuse to green scraps according to manufacturer's directions. Cut out on traced lines.

Step 3. Fuse green rectangle to pocket piece. Fold green fabric back over navy pocket front 1" and stitch with zigzag stitch and navy thread.

Step 4. Trace 4" x 10" rectangle on paper side of fusible transfer web. Cut out roughly ½" around traced lines. Fuse to a 5" x 11" rectangle of blue flannel. Cut out on traced line and fuse to shirt front, referring to photo for position. Zigzag around panel with matching thread.

Step 5. Fuse three trees to blue panel and one to pocket. Zigzag around each tree with navy thread. Create a tree trunk for each tree with satin stitch.

Step 6. From blue flannel cut two skirt pieces 40" x 34" (length). Sew pocket to front of one skirt piece with zigzag stitch and navy thread.

Step 7. Right sides together, sew the skirt pieces

Continued on page 85

TUMBLING SNOWMEN VEST

By Connie Matricardi

Start with a ready-made vest, add a flurry of frosty snowmen and wear this vest faster than you would have thought possible.

Project Specifications
Skill Level: Beginner
Vest Size: Any size

Materials
- Black wool felt vest
- 2 white wool felt rectangles 9" x 12"
- Scraps of orange wool felt
- 1¼ yards red lining fabric
- Scraps of red, green, blue and yellow small prints for appliqué scarves
- Scraps of fusible transfer web
- All-purpose threads to match fabrics
- Red, green, black and blue 6-strand embroidery floss

- 1 package of 10mm white sequins
- 1 package 4mm opaque multicolor beads
- Rocaille beads
- Craft glue
- Air-soluble marker
- White marking pencil
- Basic sewing supplies and tools

Instructions

Step 1. Carefully rip open shoulder seams of felt vest. Use the one-piece felt vest as a pattern to cut vest lining from red lining fabric. Right sides together, sew lining front to lining back at shoulder seams. Press seams open.

Step 2. Right sides together, sew vest front to vest back at shoulder seams. Press shoulder seams open.

Step 3. Right sides together, pin vest to lining at neck, front and bottom edges. Do not pin armholes. Using a ½" seam allowance, sew vest to lining. Turn right side out and press. Using a ¼" seam allowance, topstitch around neck, front, and bottom edges of vest.

Step 4. Turn raw edges of vest armhole and lining armhole under ½" and press; clip curves. Pin vest armhole to lining armhole and sew with a ¼" seam allowance. Repeat for second armhole.

Step 5. Trace and cut snowmen as directed on pattern.

Step 6. Trace scarf patterns on paper side of fusible transfer web. Cut out shapes leaving ¼" margin around. Fuse each pair of scarf pieces on eight different small print fabrics. Cut out on traced lines; fuse to snowmen.

Step 7. Cut and glue orange nose to each snowman head.

Step 8. Sew two black beads to each snowman head for eyes. Sew two colored beads to snowman body for buttons.

Step 9. With air-soluble marker draw a smiling mouth on each snowman head. With two strands of black embroidery floss, embroider mouth line with a running stitch.

Step 10. Using photo as a guide, position and pin snowman shapes to vest front. With 3 strands of embroidery floss, buttonhole-stitch snowman shapes in place. Avoid catching lining fabric in buttonhole stitch.

Step 11. Using photo as a guide, position sequins on vest front. Mark the position of the sequins with white marking pencil. Sew sequins to vest front using one rocaille bead for each sequin.

Step 12. With 6 strands of red embroidery floss, work buttonhole stitch around neck, front and bottom edge of vest, and around each armhole. ❅

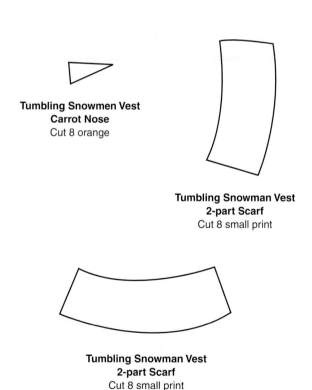

Tumbling Snowmen Vest
Carrot Nose
Cut 8 orange

Tumbling Snowman Vest
2-part Scarf
Cut 8 small print

Tumbling Snowman Vest
2-part Scarf
Cut 8 small print

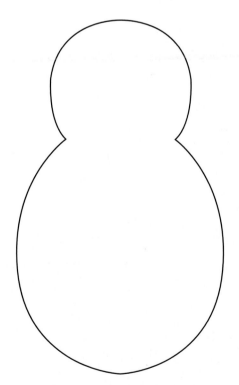

Tumbling Snowmen Vest
Snowman
Cut 8 white felt

TWINKLE, TWINKLE LITTLE ANGEL VEST

By Janice Loewenthal

The shape of these angels conforms perfectly to the points on the vest for a special custom-made look.

Project Specifications
Skill Level: Beginner
Vest Size: Any size

Materials
- Commercial vest pattern with hemline front points
- Fabric as indicated on pattern for size
- Assortment of fabric scraps for appliqué
- Scraps of fusible transfer web
- Scraps of fabric stabilizer
- Machine-appliqué threads to coordinate with appliqué fabrics
- All-purpose thread to match vest fabric
- Black .05mm permanent marker
- White acrylic paint
- Paintbrush
- Powdered blush
- Cotton swab
- Basic sewing supplies and tools

Instructions
Step 1. Cut out vest and lining.

Step 2. Adjust bottom portion of angel's gown to match points on vest pattern.

Step 3. Trace appliqué shapes on paper side of fusible transfer web. Cut out leaving ½" margin around shapes. Fuse to selected fabrics following manufacturer's directions. Cut out on traced lines.

Twinkle, Twinkle Little Angel Vest
Face
Cut 1

Twinkle, Twinkle Little Angel Vest
Gown
Cut 1

Twinkle, Twinkle Little Angel Vest
Hands
Cut 2 (reverse 1)

Twinkle, Twinkle Little Angel Vest
Hair
Cut 1

Step 4. Referring to photo, arrange appliqués on vest fronts; fuse.

Step 5. Cut pieces of stabilizer slightly larger than design areas. Place under fabric and stitch around each appliqué piece with satin stitch. Remove stabilizer and clip threads.

Step 6. Complete vest construction according to pattern instructions.

Step 7. Draw angels' facial features with black permanent marker. Make highlights in eyes with white acrylic paint. Brush cheeks lightly with cotton swab and powdered blush. ✲

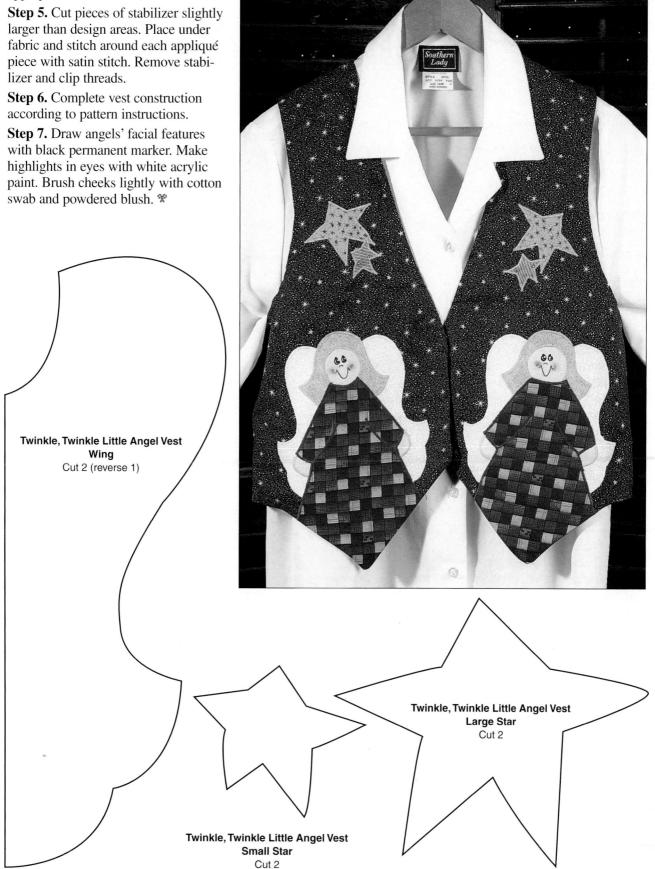

**Twinkle, Twinkle Little Angel Vest
Wing**
Cut 2 (reverse 1)

**Twinkle, Twinkle Little Angel Vest
Large Star**
Cut 2

**Twinkle, Twinkle Little Angel Vest
Small Star**
Cut 2

HOLIDAY HOSTESS APRON

By Joanne S. Bembry

With fusible appliqué techniques, this holiday apron can quickly be made in multiples for giving to all on your gift list.

Project Specifications
Skill Level: Beginner
Apron Size: All sizes

Materials
- Scraps of solid and white print and 6 or more red and green holiday prints
- Ready-made chef's apron, any size
- Scraps of fusible transfer web
- ½ yard each ⅛"-wide red and green satin ribbon
- All-purpose white thread
- 6-strand gold metallic embroidery floss
- Fabric protection spray, optional
- Basic sewing supplies and tools

Instructions
Step 1. On paper side of fusible transfer web draw two rectangles 5½" x 4" and four rectangles 2¾" x 5".

Step 2. Following manufacturer's directions, fuse two 2¾" x 5" rectangles to solid white fabric. Fuse remaining rectangles to red or green prints.

Step 3. Trace appliqué shapes onto paper side of fusible transfer web. Cut around each shape leaving roughly ½" margin. Referring to photo for ideas, fuse to selected fabrics and cut out on traced lines.

Step 4. Position appliqué pieces on fabric rectangles and fuse.

Step 5. Measure and center a 9" x 11" rectangle on bib portion of apron. Position fused blocks within rectangle referring to the photo for placement. With white thread, machine satin-stitch around each fused block and around outside of entire rectangle.

Step 6. Referring to photo, trim packages and gingerbread men with red and green satin ribbons.

Step 7. For protection against soil and stains, spray appliqué with fabric protection spray. ❀

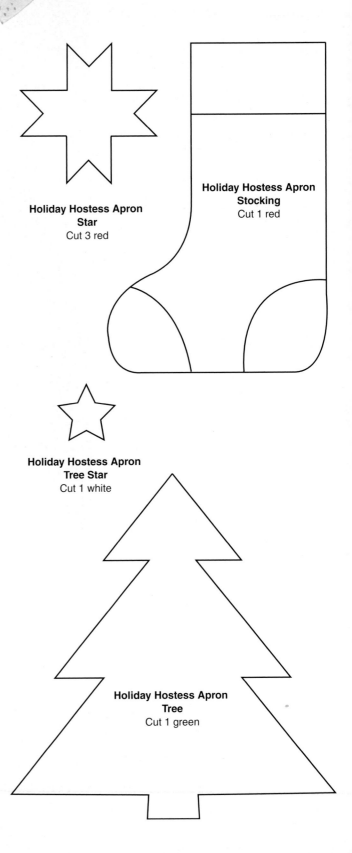

Holiday Hostess Apron Star
Cut 3 red

Holiday Hostess Apron Stocking
Cut 1 red

Holiday Hostess Apron Tree Star
Cut 1 white

Holiday Hostess Apron Tree
Cut 1 green

Holiday Hostess Apron
Package 1
Cut 1 red

Holiday Hostess Apron
Package 2
Cut 1 white

Holiday Hostess Apron
Package 3
Cut 1 green

Patterns continued on page 85

HOLLY BUTTONS CHRISTMAS OUTFIT

By June Fiechter

Different popovers could add endless variety to this basic dress. Create a new one for every holiday.

Project Specifications
Skill Level: Beginner
Dress Size: Pattern for sizes 3–8

Materials
- Commercial pattern New Look Easy 6850 by Simplicity
- Off-white Dress C fabric as required for size
- Red plaid Popover D fabric as required for size
- ½ yard green plaid for trim and appliqué
- 10 (⅜") wooden buttons
- 1 yard ¼"-wide black ribbon
- Zipper for Dress C as required on pattern
- All-purpose threads to match fabrics
- Scraps of fusible transfer web
- Basic sewing supplies and tools

Instructions

BASIC DRESS C

Step 1. When pinning pattern piece 6 to fabric, fold right side of pattern in 7" (eliminating 14" from back of skirt). Cut according to directions on pattern.

Step 2. Repeat Step 1 for skirt front using pattern piece 5.

Step 3. When pinning sleeve to fabric add 4¼" to length. Cut as directed.

Step 4. Place pattern piece 3 on green plaid fabric, pin and cut.

Step 5. Cut bodice front and back and sew all pieces according to directions.

Step 6. From green plaid fabric cut two pieces each 2¼" x 11" for cuffs. Stitch to lower edge of sleeves.

POPOVER DRESS D

Step 1. When cutting skirt back, pattern piece 6, place center back seam of skirt on fold and cut one piece, eliminating 11" from right side (equaling 22" total on width of skirt back).

Step 2. Repeat Step 1 for skirt front using pattern piece 5.

Step 3. When cutting bodice, match plaid with skirt and cut according to directions.

Step 4. Trace holly on paper side of fusible web as directed on pattern. Cut out ½" beyond traced lines. Fuse to green plaid according to manufacturer's directions. Cut out on traced lines. Using photo as a placement guide, fuse to skirt and bodice.

Step 5. With machine zigzag stitch finish edges of holly. Sew buttons between leaves—three on bodice and two each on skirt.

Step 6. Hem bottom edge of skirt front and back. Turn under narrow hem on both sides of skirt front and back; stitch. Measure up 8½" from bottom of skirt front and back and stitch ¼"-wide black ribbon in place.

Step 7. Cut a 4" slit from waist down center of skirt back. From red plaid cut a bias strip 9" x 1¼". Bind slit with bias strip.

Step 8. Sew a ½" x 3½" dart, placing each dart 3½" to each side of center opening.

Step 9. Sew bodice according to pattern directions, replacing zipper with three buttons. Attach skirt back to bodice, matching openings at center. Attach skirt front to bodice front, matching plaid pattern.

Step 10. Finish inside as directed in pattern. ❦

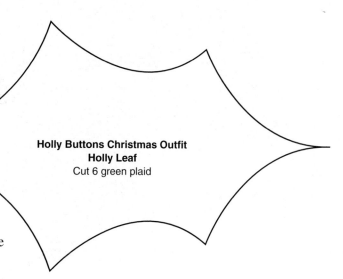

Holly Buttons Christmas Outfit
Holly Leaf
Cut 6 green plaid

SNOWMEN ON PARADE

By Julie Weaver

Every snowman has personality and this sweatshirt parade offers eight charming snow guys and gals to cheer your holiday.

Project Specifications
Skill Level: Beginner
Sweatshirt Size: Any size

Materials
- Black sweatshirt in size of your choice
- ¾ yard plaid or check flannel
- ⅓ yard muslin for snowmen
- Scraps of fusible transfer web
- Scraps of fusible interfacing
- Scraps of flannel for clothing appliqué
- Ecru, red and orange fine-line permanent markers
- Ecru, gray and brown 6-strand embroidery floss
- 16 (⅜"–½") buttons
- Basic sewing supplies and tools

Note: Prewash sweatshirt and all fabrics; ¼" seams used throughout.

Instructions
Step 1. Cut sleeve, bottom and neck ribbing from sweatshirt. Cut opening down center front. If you would like to reduce bulk in your jacket, trim an equal amount from each side of center front opening. Stay-stitch neckline.

Step 2. From plaid or check flannel cut

and piece enough 2½"-wide bias to make a 160" length. Press wrong sides together lengthwise. Pin raw edges to right side of jacket bottom, front and neckline; stitch. Turn binding to inside and slipstitch in place by hand.

Step 3. Sew a gathering stitch around bottom of each sleeve. From the plaid or check flannel cut, on the bias, two cuffs 7" x 12½". Cut two pieces of fusible interfacing 3½" x 12½". Fuse interfacing to one half of wrong side of each cuff piece. Press under a ¼" hem on the other half of the cuff pieces. With right sides together sew the side seam on each cuff.

Step 4. With right sides together, pin cuffs to the jacket, using the gathering stitches to ease in fullness if necessary; stitch. Turn cuffs to the inside and slipstitch in place over sewn seam. When finished, turn cuff up on outside of jacket.

Step 5. Trace appliqué shapes on paper side of fusible transfer web as directed on patterns. Cut out leaving a ½" margin around traced lines. Following manufacturer's instructions, fuse to selected fabrics and cut out on traced lines. Lightly trace facial features on snowmen with pencil.

Continued on page 85

Left Front

Back

Right Front

Fig. 1
Arrange snowmen on front and back vest as shown.
Place clothing, arms and buttons on snowmen as indicated.

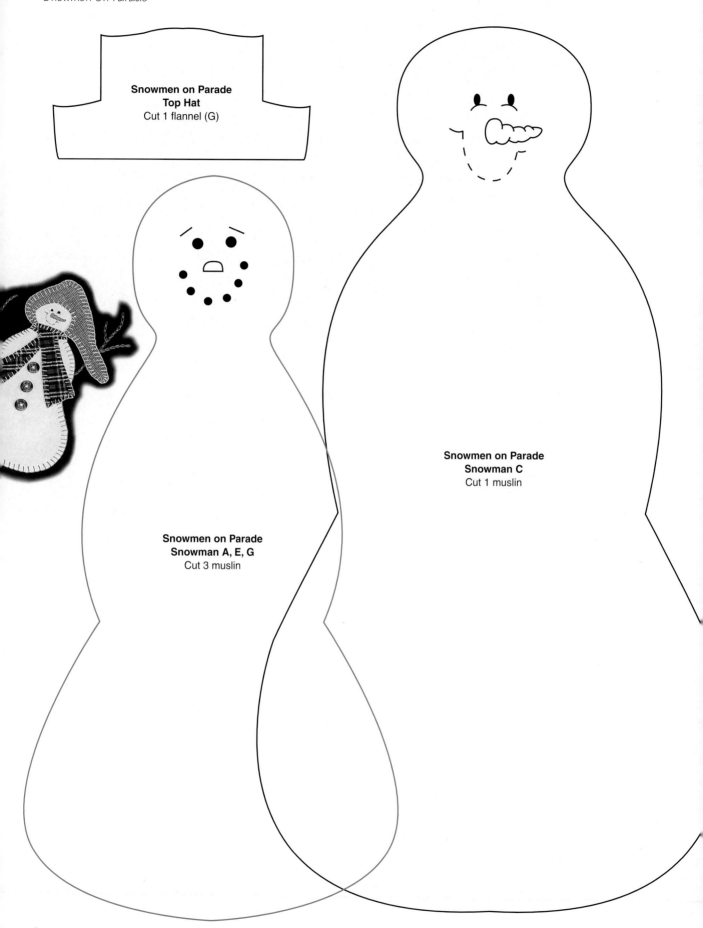

Snowmen on Parade
Top Hat
Cut 1 flannel (G)

Snowmen on Parade
Snowman C
Cut 1 muslin

Snowmen on Parade
Snowman A, E, G
Cut 3 muslin

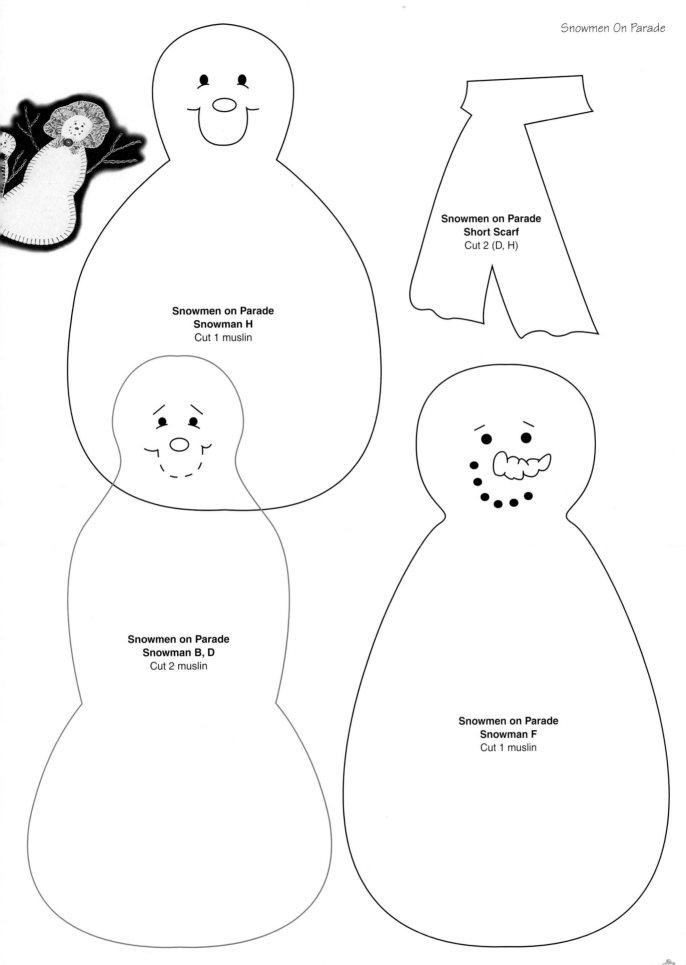

**Snowmen on Parade
Short Scarf**
Cut 2 (D, H)

**Snowmen on Parade
Snowman H**
Cut 1 muslin

**Snowmen on Parade
Snowman B, D**
Cut 2 muslin

**Snowmen on Parade
Snowman F**
Cut 1 muslin

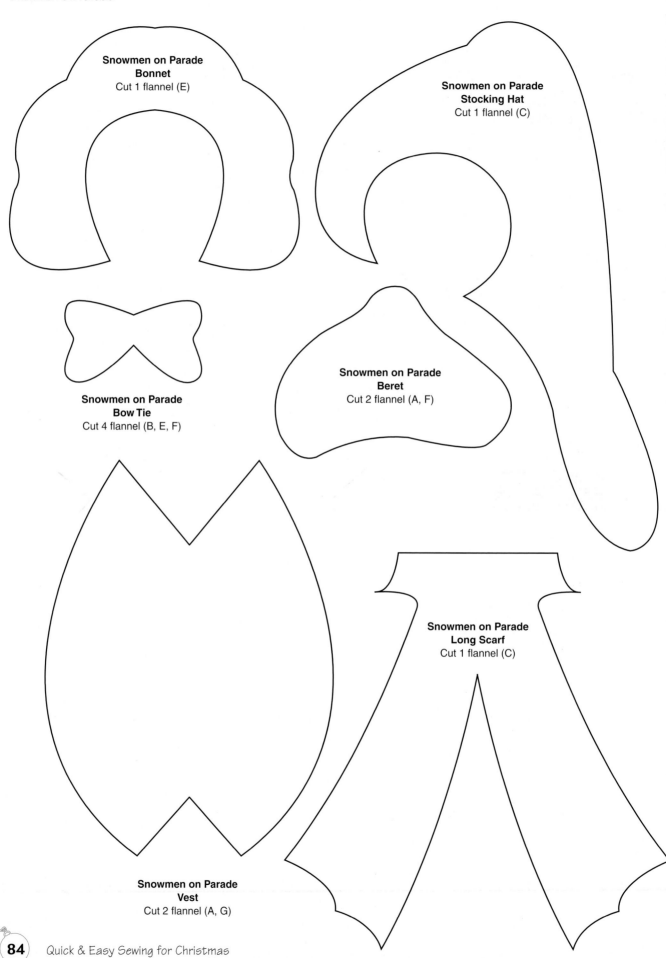

**Snowmen on Parade
Bonnet**
Cut 1 flannel (E)

**Snowmen on Parade
Stocking Hat**
Cut 1 flannel (C)

**Snowmen on Parade
Bow Tie**
Cut 4 flannel (B, E, F)

**Snowmen on Parade
Beret**
Cut 2 flannel (A, F)

**Snowmen on Parade
Long Scarf**
Cut 1 flannel (C)

**Snowmen on Parade
Vest**
Cut 2 flannel (A, G)

Step 6. Position snowmen along jacket bottom, referring to Fig. 1 and photo. Fuse in place. Arrange scarves, hats and vests on snowmen; fuse.

Step 7. With 3 strands of ecru embroidery floss, work buttonhole stitch around each article of clothing. With gray embroidery floss, buttonhole-stitch around snowmen.

Step 8. With 6 strands of brown embroidery floss, chain-stitch twig arms on each snowman as shown in Fig. 1.

Step 9. With black fine-line permanent marker, trace facial features. Fill in round noses with red marker and carrot noses with orange.

Step 10. Position buttons on each showman as shown in Fig. 1; sew in place to finish. ❄

Trio of Trees Dress
Continued from page 71

together at the sides. Hem bottom of skirt. Gather top edge of skirt, pin to bottom of T-shirt and sew in place.

Step 8. Sew star button to top of center tree. ❄

**Trio of Trees Dress
Tree**
Cut 4 green print

Holiday Hostess Apron
Continued from page 77

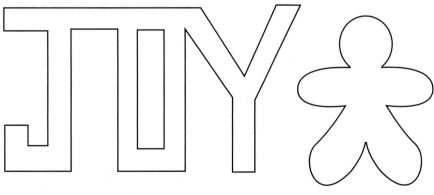

**Holiday Hostess Apron
Joy**
Cut 1 green

**Holiday Hostess Apron
Gingerbread Men**
Cut 3 white

ALL DECKED OUT

Instead of boughs of holly, deck the halls of your home with some of these festive sewing projects.

A heart-adorned valance hanging in your window will welcome visitors with warmth and cheer, and gold stars will shine on your holiday table. All these and more await you in this chapter!

All of these projects are quick and easy, which means you can stitch up a few while your Christmas cookies are baking!

COUNTRY CHRISTMAS HEARTS VALANCE

By Chris Malone

Decorate the window that frames your favorite view with this simple but warm-hearted holiday valance.

Project Specifications

Skill Level: Beginner

Valance Size: Approximately 44" x 14"

Note: Materials and instructions are for a window 30" wide. Add or subtract squares to adjust for other window sizes.

Materials

- Variety of green print scraps
- Variety of natural and tan print scraps
- Variety of red scraps
- ¼ yard red print for borders
- ½ yard muslin for lining
- Scraps of fusible transfer web
- Black 6-strand embroidery floss
- 11 (⅝") red buttons
- 7 (1¼") tan buttons
- Embroidery needle
- Rotary-cutting tools
- Basic sewing supplies and tools

Instructions

Step 1. From tan and natural prints rotary-cut 28 squares 2½" x 2½" and from green prints cut 35 squares 2½" x 2½". Assemble and sew seven Nine-Patch blocks as shown in Fig. 1. Press seams toward green blocks in rows and outward from the center when joining rows.

Fig. 1
Sew Nine-Patch blocks as shown.

Step 2. Trace hearts on paper side of fusible transfer web as directed on patterns. Cut out leaving roughly ½" margin around traced lines. Following manufacturer's directions, fuse to selected red scraps. Cut out on traced lines.

Step 3. From tan and natural prints cut seven squares 6½" x 6½". Center one heart on each square and fuse in

Country Christmas Hearts Valance
Heart
Cut 7 red

place. With two strands of black embroidery floss, work a buttonhole stitch around each heart.

Step 4. Arrange blocks as shown in Fig. 2 and sew together.

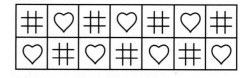

Fig. 2
Arrange blocks as shown.

Step 5. Cut two red strips each 1½" x 44½" (piece if necessary) and 1½" x 12½". Sew shorter strips to sides of valance and longer strips to top and bottom. Press seams toward borders.

Step 6. From green print scraps cut 11 strips 2½" x 6".

GINGERBREAD GRINS PILLOW

By June Fiechter

Sugar and spice, giggles and grins all come to mind when you create this little gingerbread boy on his own soft pillow.

Project Specifications

Skill Level: Beginner
Pillow Size: 15" x 15"

Materials

- Green textured felt 30½" x 15½"
- Red textured felt 11" x 11"
- Tan plush felt 7" x 10"
- Green textured felt scrap for scarf
- 2 (¼") black buttons
- 3 (½") burgundy buttons
- 11" piece of white trim or shoelace
- Scraps of fusible transfer web
- All-purpose threads to match fabrics
- Black all-purpose thread
- Medium-weight batting 7" x 10"
- Pillow form 15" x 15"
- Basic sewing supplies and tools

Instructions

Step 1. Trace scarf and gingerbread boy onto paper side of fusible transfer web. Cut out leaving roughly ½" beyond traced lines. Following manufacturer's directions fuse to selected fabrics. Cut out on traced lines.

Step 2. Trace mouth on gingerbread boy. Satin-stitch over traced lines with black thread. With green thread, satin-stitch neck portion of scarf in place.

Step 3. Referring to photo for placement, sew two black buttons on face for eyes and three burgundy buttons on body front. Sew white trim in place.

Step 4. Cut an 11" x 11" square of fusible transfer web and fuse to wrong side of red textured felt square.

Step 5. Fold the textured green felt in half, wrong sides together, to form a square. Center the fusible side of the red textured square on one side of folded green felt and fuse in place.

Step 6. Cut one gingerbread boy from batting ¼" smaller all around than pattern and center on red felt square. Center tan gingerbread boy on top of batting; fuse. Satin-stitch around all edges with matching thread.

Step 7. Place scarf ends to right of neckline as shown in photo. Fuse and satin-stitch in place with matching green thread.

Step 8. Turn green felt with right sides together and stitch sides only. Turn right side out and insert pillow form. Turn bottom edges in and close with either hand- or machine-stitches. ✿

Continued on page 113

Country Christmas Hearts Valance

Fold each in half lengthwise, right sides together, and stitch long edge and across one end. Clip corners, turn right side out and press.

Step 7. Pin hanging tabs to top edge of valance with raw edges aligned. For even spacing place one tab above each green square of Nine-Patch blocks and one centered above each heart block. Baste in place.

Step 8. Cut muslin 14½" x 44½" (piece if necessary). With right sides together pin, and sew muslin lining to pieced valance, leaving a 7" opening along one side. Clip corners, turn right side out and press. Hand-sew opening closed.

Step 9. Fold hanging tabs to front of valance, overlapping top edge 1". Sew a red button to each tab end, sewing through all layers.

Step 10. Sew a tan button to center of each heart, sewing through all layers. ✿

CUTWORK SNOWFLAKES
MANTEL SCARF

By Karen Neary

Sparkling white and light as new-fallen snow—a perfect backdrop for Christmas candles and ornaments.

Project Specifications

Skill Level: Beginner

Mantel Scarf Size: Approximately 16" x 81"

Note: Fits mantel 7" x 64"

Materials

- 2¼ yards white-on-white print
- 2¼ yards fusible transfer web
- 2¼ yards tear-away stabilizer and 10 squares 8" x 8"
- White rayon machine-embroidery thread
- Sharp embroidery scissors
- Basic sewing supplies and tools

Instructions

Step 1. Cut white-on-white fabric 33" x 81". Cut fusible web 16½" x 81". With one long edge of each aligned and following manufacturer's instructions, fuse web to wrong side of fabric (web will cover half of fabric). Remove paper backing and fold other half of fabric over fusible transfer web, keeping raw edges together. Smooth fabric and fuse.

Step 2. Trace 10 snowflakes onto tear-away stabilizer squares. Position eight snowflakes along front of scarf on right side of fabric, placing snowflakes ½" from outside (raw) edge. Place one snowflake on each end ¼" from folded edge and ½" beyond the end of front-edge snowflakes as shown in Fig. 1. Pin in place. Using white rayon machine-embroidery thread, straight-stitch through the tear-away stabilizer, following all lines marked on design. Clip thread ends; carefully remove tear-away stabilizer.

Step 3. Referring to photo, use sharp embroidery scissors to cut out interior sections. Cut as closely as possible to stitching. Place additional tear-away stabilizer underneath work and satin-stitch over previous line of stitching using a narrow zigzag stitch. Tie and clip thread ends. Carefully remove stabilizer. Steam-press scarf.

Note: If desired, a seam sealant may be applied to cut edges and clipped thread ends. ❆

Pattern continued on page 112

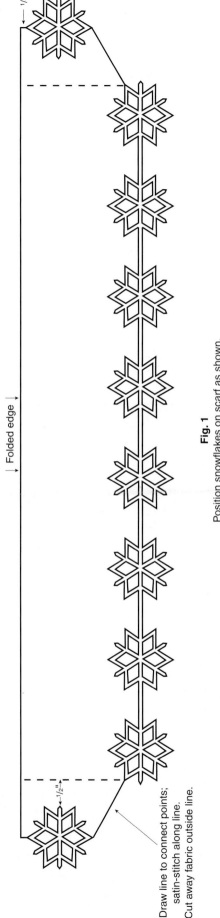

Folded edge

1/4"

1/2"

Draw line to connect points;
satin-stitch along line.
Cut away fabric outside line.

Fig. 1
Position snowflakes on scarf as shown.

HERE COMES SANTA PILLOW

By Chris Malone

Not exactly "redwork," but you'll recognize a more colorful version of that recently revived form of stitchery in this embroidered Santa.

Project Specifications
Skill Level: Beginner
Pillow Size: Approximately 14" x 14"

Materials
- ⅓ yard plain white fabric
- ⅛ yard green print
- ½ yard red Christmas print
- Black, red, gray, green, gold, blue and brown 6-strand embroidery floss (or colors that coordinate with your selected Christmas print)
- 2 (3mm) black beads
- 1 (4mm) red bead
- 5 (½") matching or assorted red buttons
- 6" pieces of red, blue and gold ¼"-wide grosgrain ribbon
- 1⅓ yards 1"-wide red grosgrain ribbon
- 4 (¾") white buttons
- 14" x 14" pillow form
- Air-soluble marker or sharp pencil
- Embroidery needle
- 8" embroidery hoop
- 14" x 14" piece of cardboard
- All-purpose threads to match fabrics
- Fabric glue
- Basic sewing supplies and tools

Instructions
Step 1. From white fabric cut a 12" x 12" square. Trace embroidery pattern with air-soluble marker or sharp pencil. (Remember that air-soluble marker will fade within 12 hours.)

Step 2. Place fabric in embroidery hoop and backstitch lines with two strands of embroidery floss, referring to photo for color placement. Remove from hoop and press. Trim block to 8½" x 8½".

Step 3. From green print cut two strips each 1" x 8½" and 1" x 9½". Sew shorter strips to sides of embroidered block and longer strips to top and bottom. Press seams toward borders.

Step 4. From red Christmas print cut two strips each 3" x 9½" and 3" x 14½". Sew shorter strips to sides and longer strips to top and bottom. Press seams toward borders.

Step 5. From red Christmas print cut two rectangles 9" x 14½". Stitch a doubled ¼" hem along one short edge of each piece.

Step 6. Overlap 14½" edges of backing rectangles and place right sides

**Here Comes Santa Pillow
Embroidery Pattern**

together with pillow front. Stitch all around edges. Trim corners and turn right side out.

Step 7. Slip cardboard piece inside pillow cover while adding embellishments to prevent sewing pillow front to pillow back. Referring to photo for placement, sew black beads in place for eyes and red bead for nose. Sew two black buttons on front of Santa's robe and five red buttons to Christmas tree.

Step 8. Tie each 6" grosgrain ribbon length in a bow and sew or glue to packages.

Step 9. Cut red grosgrain ribbon into four 12" pieces. Place a pin 2¼" from each end of one ribbon and one pin at center. Fold each end back and match pins at center. Hold in place and remove pins. Sew gathering stitches down center of bow with white thread; pull gathers tight, wrap thread around center two times and knot. Sew a white button to center of bow. Repeat for four bows.

Step 10. Sew or glue a bow to each corner of pillow front. Insert pillow form. ❀

TWINKLING STAR PLACE MATS

By Charlyne Stewart

Twinkle, twinkle little star, how you brighten everything—Christmas and all special occasions!

Project Specifications
Skill Level: Beginner
Place Mat Size: Approximately 18½" x 11½"

Materials
Note: Materials and instructions are for two place mats.

- ¾ yard green metallic print
- ¾ yard thin batting
- Scraps of gold fabric
- Scraps of fusible transfer web
- Green all-purpose sewing thread
- Gold metallic thread
- 20" x 13" pattern paper
- Basic sewing supplies and tools

Instructions
Step 1. Trace pattern, placing folds as instructed.

Step 2. Using paper pattern, for each place mat cut two fabric ovals and one batting oval.

Step 3. Place two fabric ovals right sides together. Place batting oval on top. Pin together and sew with ½" seam allowance, leaving a 3" opening for turning.

Step 4. Turn right side out and close opening with hand stitches; press. Repeat for two place mats.

Step 5. Trace two stars on paper side of fusible transfer web. Cut out leaving roughly ½" margin around traced lines. Following manufacturer's directions, fuse to gold scraps. Cut out on traced lines.

Step 6. Referring to photo, place stars on place mats and fuse. Draw lines radiating to edges. Machine-appliqué with a medium satin stitch around star and on lines with gold metallic thread in needle and green all-purpose thread in bobbin. Repeat with a slightly wider stitch. Trim loose threads. ❊

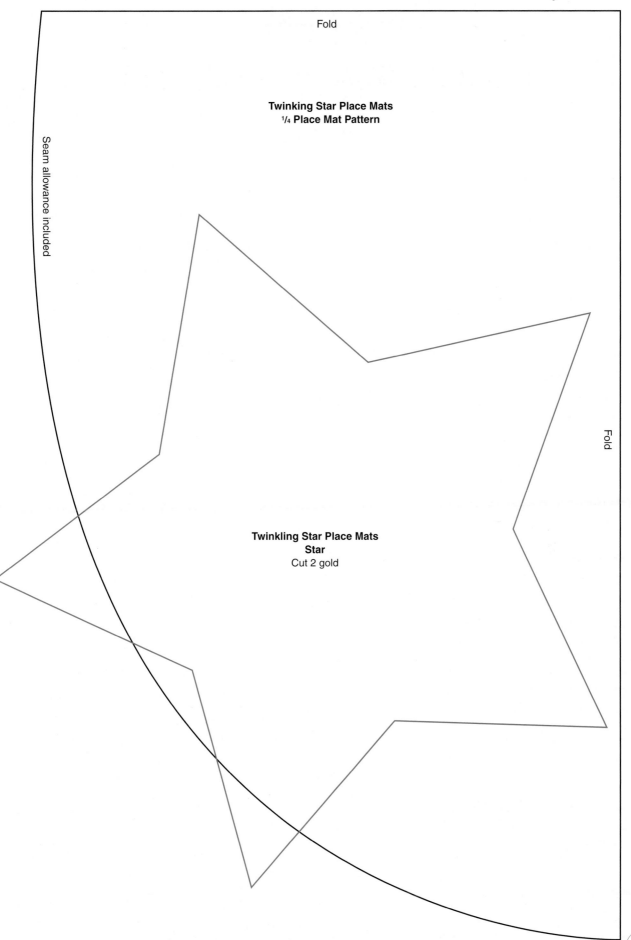

Fold

Twinking Star Place Mats
1/4 Place Mat Pattern

Seam allowance included

Fold

Twinkling Star Place Mats
Star
Cut 2 gold

HOLLY DREAMS SHEET SET

By Jill Reber

Holiday linens are special indeed! They will surely bring sweet dreams of Christmas to anyone sleeping upon them.

Project Specifications

Skill Level: Beginner

Sheet Size: Double

Pillowcase Size: Standard

Note: Materials and instructions are for one double flat sheet and two standard pillowcases. Increase or decrease number of appliqués for other sizes.

Materials

- 1 double flat sheet
- 2 standard pillowcases
- Scraps of green prints for holly leaves
- 13 assorted red buttons
- Scraps of fusible transfer web
- Red pearl cotton
- Green machine-appliqué thread
- Basic sewing supplies and tools

Instructions

SHEET

Step 1. Trace 11 holly leaves on paper side of fusible transfer web (adjusting number for larger or smaller sheet). Cut out leaving roughly ½" margin around traced lines. Following manufacturer's directions, fuse to selected green scraps. Cut out on traced lines.

Step 2. Arrange holly leaves along top hem of sheet as shown in Fig. 1. Fuse in place. Add red buttons and tie in place with red pearl cotton.

PILLOWCASES

Step 1. Following Sheet, Step 1 instructions, trace six holly leaves for two standard pillowcases. Referring to Fig. 2, arrange on pillowcases and fuse.

Step 2. Add red buttons and tie in place with red pearl cotton. ❀

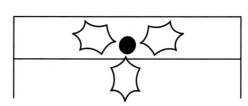

Fig. 1
Arrange holly leaves on sheet as shown.

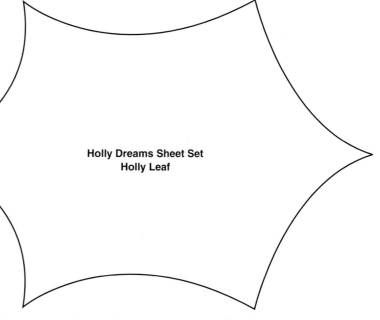

Fig. 2
Arrange holly leaves on pillowcase as shown.

**Holly Dreams Sheet Set
Holly Leaf**

SEASONS GREETINGS MAILBOX COVER

By Janice Loewenthal

Everyone—including the mailman—will enjoy this creation for a well-dressed mailbox.

Project Specifications
Skill Level: Beginner
Mailbox Cover Size: Approximately 17½" x 21"

Materials
- ⅔ yard green cotton duck
- Variety of scraps for appliqué
- Scraps of fusible transfer web
- Scraps of fabric stabilizer
- All-purpose threads to match fabrics
- Fine-line permanent black marker
- Powdered blush
- Cotton swab
- Basic sewing supplies and tools

Instructions
Step 1. From green cotton duck cut two rectangles 18" x 21½".

Step 2. Trace appliqués on paper side of fusible transfer web as directed on patterns. Cut out leaving roughly ½" margin around traced lines. Following manufacturer's directions, fuse to selected fabrics. Cut out on traced lines.

Step 3. Referring to photo, arrange appliqué pieces on one side of one green rectangle, leaving enough room at bottom for ¼" seam allowance. Repeat on the other side. Fuse in place.

Step 4. Cut a piece of fabric stabilizer slightly larger than the design area and place on underside of fabric. Satin-stitch around appliqués with matching threads. Stitch lettering on envelope. Remove stabilizer and clip loose threads.

Step 5. From green cotton duck cut six strips 18½" x 2". Fold strips in half lengthwise, right sides together. Stitch along outer edge and across one end. Turn right side out; press. Position three straps on right side of each long side of appliquéd mailbox cover as shown in Fig. 1. Raw edges of strips should be aligned with raw edges of cover.

Step 6. With straps folded toward center, place right side of lining piece to right side of cover. Stitch around outer edge leaving an opening on one end for turning.

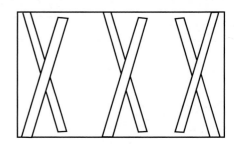

Fig. 1
Place 6 straps as shown.

Turn right side out and press.

Step 7. Turn edges of opening under and press. Topstitch close to outer edge all around mailbox cover.

Step 8. With fine-line permanent black marker, draw facial features. With cotton swab and powdered blush, give Santa's cheeks a rosy glow. Dry thoroughly; press to permanently set. ❦

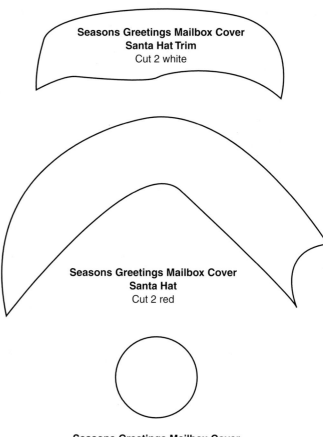

Seasons Greetings Mailbox Cover
Santa Hat Trim
Cut 2 white

Seasons Greetings Mailbox Cover
Santa Hat
Cut 2 red

Seasons Greetings Mailbox Cover
Hat Tassel
Cut 2 white

Seasons Greetings Mailbox Cover
Santa Face
Cut 2 flesh-tone

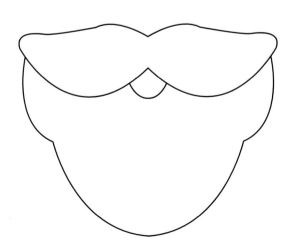

Seasons Greetings Mailbox Cover
Santa Beard
Cut 2 white

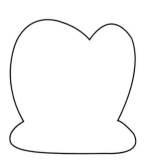

Seasons Greetings Mailbox Cover
Santa Gloves
Cut 4 black
(reverse 2)

Seasons Greetings Mailbox Cover
Heart
Cut 4 red stripe

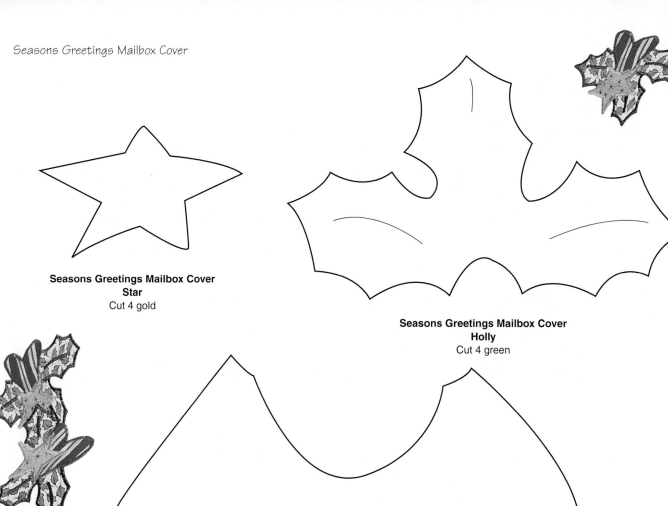

**Seasons Greetings Mailbox Cover
Star**
Cut 4 gold

**Seasons Greetings Mailbox Cover
Holly**
Cut 4 green

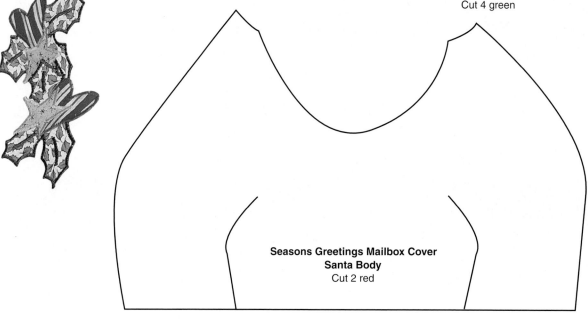

**Seasons Greetings Mailbox Cover
Santa Body**
Cut 2 red

Letter Background—Cut 2 red stripe

Seasons
Greetings

**Seasons Greetings Mailbox Cover
Letter Front**
Cut 2 white

TUMBLING STARS PLACE MAT SET

By June Fiechter

Start with a ready-made place mat, add some homespun embellishment, napkin and matching napkin ring and your holiday table will sparkle with stars and hospitality.

Project Specifications
Skill Level: Beginner
Place Mat Size: Approximately 17" x 12½"
Napkin Size: 17" x 17"
Napkin Ring Size: 1" x 1½"

Materials
Note: Materials and instructions are for one place mat, one napkin and one napkin ring.

For Place Mat
- Oval muslin place mat from Bag Works
- 12 homespun squares 5" x 5" in blue, red and green
- 6 (½") natural buttons

For Napkin Ring
- 1" x 1½" cardboard ring (cut from toilet tissue tube)
- 2 squares blue homespun 5" x 5"
- 1 square red homespun 5" x 2"
- 2 (½") natural buttons
- Fabric glue

For Napkin
- 2 squares green homespun 18" x 18"

For Place Mat, Napkin & Napkin Ring
- Scraps 5" x 5" fusible transfer web
- All-purpose threads to match fabrics
- Basic sewing supplies and tools

Instructions

PLACE MAT

Step 1. Trace stars on paper side of fusible transfer web as directed on pattern. Cut out leaving roughly ½" margin around traced lines. Following manufacturer's directions fuse to selected fabrics. Cut out on traced lines.

Step 2. Referring to photo arrange stars randomly around edges of place mat. Trim edges to conform to place-mat edges, reapplying cut-off points over and between stars. Tuck edges of stars under bias binding. Fuse in place.

Step 3. Zigzag around stars with matching threads. Attach buttons randomly, referring to photo.

NAPKIN RING

Step 1. Wrap red homespun around cardboard ring and glue in place with fabric glue.

Step 2. Trace stars on paper side of fusible transfer web as directed on pattern. Cut out leaving roughly ½" margin around traced lines. Following manufacturer's directions fuse to blue homespun. Cut out on traced lines. Fuse wrong sides together. Zigzag around edges with matching thread.

Step 3. Attach two buttons to center of star and glue star to ring with fabric glue.

NAPKIN

Step 1. Right sides together, sew green homespun squares together on three sides. Turn right side out and press.

Step 2. Fold open edges of napkin under ¼"; press. Topstitch around all edges of napkin. ❦

Tumbling Stars Place Mat Set
Place Mat
Cut 12 red, blue and green homespun

Napkin Ring
Cut 2 blue homespun

CHRISTMAS WRAP ORGANIZER

By Pat Everson

Vertical pockets for rolls of wrapping paper and a yardstick, and horizontal pockets for scissors, pens, pencils, flat-fold wrap and your address book—everything at your fingertips for the final rush.

Project Specifications
Skill Level: Beginner
Wrap Organizer Size: Approximately 16½" x 32" (excluding plastic hanger)

Materials
- 1 yard solid red fabric
- ¼ yard solid green fabric
- ½ yard novelty Christmas print
- 1 package red extra-wide double-fold bias binding
- 1 package green extra-wide double-fold bias binding
- 1 red or green plastic coat hanger
- 7 (1") red or green buttons
- Red and green all-purpose thread
- Basic sewing supplies and tools

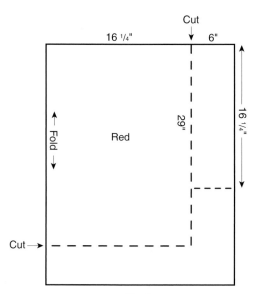

Fig. 1
Cut panel on fold as shown,
then cut 1 piece 6" x 16 ¼" from
remaining fabric.

Instructions

Step 1. Fold red fabric selvage edges together. Measure 16¼" in from folded edge and mark. Measure down length of fabric 29". Cut out folded piece as shown in Fig. 1. From remaining fabric cut one rectangle 16¼" x 6". Fold in half lengthwise; press both long edges to the center fold to make an extra-wide piece of binding.

Step 2. From extra-wide green bias binding cut a 32½" piece and sew, as shown in Fig. 2, to one end of folded red panel cut in Step 1.

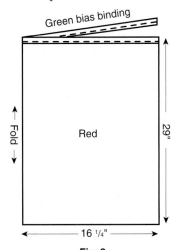

Fig. 2
Sew binding to folded panel as shown.

Step 3. From Christmas novelty print cut a rectangle 16¼" x 25¾". From extra-wide green bias binding cut a 16¼" piece and bind top of Christmas print rectangle as shown in Fig. 3.

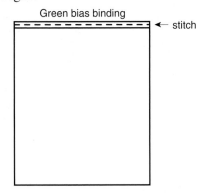

Fig. 3
Bind panel as shown.

Step 4. Place Christmas print panel on top of red

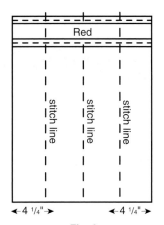

Fig. 4
Mark and stitch vertical lines as shown.

panel, aligning bottom unbound edges. Mark center top and mark 4¼" in from both outside edges. Mark the same three places on lower edge. Draw a light pencil line joining top and bottom marks. Stitch on lines as shown in Fig. 4.

Step 5. From green fabric cut a rectangle 16¼" x 8". Slip one long edge into red binding strip cut in Step 1, topstitch.

Step 6. Place green panel on top of panels sewn in Step 4, aligning lower edges. Mark center bottom and draw a line from previously marked center top to center bottom. Stitch on line.

Step 7. Pin extra-wide red bias binding to sides and bottom of holder and stitch in place.

Step 8. From novelty Christmas print cut four strips 8½" x 4". Right sides facing, fold each in half lengthwise and sew long edge and one short end with ¼" seam allowance. Turn right side out and press. Fold corners in on short finished ends to form points. Hand-stitch in place.

Step 9. Referring to photo for placement, pin unfinished ends of straps to wrong side of front layer of red fabric. Turn in raw edges and stitch straps to bias binding on previous stitching line. Do not stitch through both red layers or you will not be able to use the pockets intended for wrapping paper.

Step 10. Wrap straps over coat hanger and stitch each to bias binding on previous stitching line.

Step 11. Sew buttons to pointed ends of straps and on bottom pocket, referring to photo for placement. ❊

POINSETTIA HOT MATS

By Phyllis M. Dobbs

Go ahead! Put your oven-hot dish on any serving surface and fear no spots or rings. This pretty hot mat will provide great protection and it's holiday festive as well.

Project Specifications
Skill Level: Beginner
Hot Mat Size: Approximately 11½" x 11½"

Materials
Note: Materials are for two mats.
- ⅓ yard red print fabric
- ⅓ yard green print fabric
- Scraps of gold and four or more different red prints
- ⅓ yard cotton batting (Polyester may melt with heat.)
- 1 package red glass E beads, size 6/0
- Scraps of fusible transfer web
- Red, gold and green all-purpose thread
- Basic sewing supplies and tools

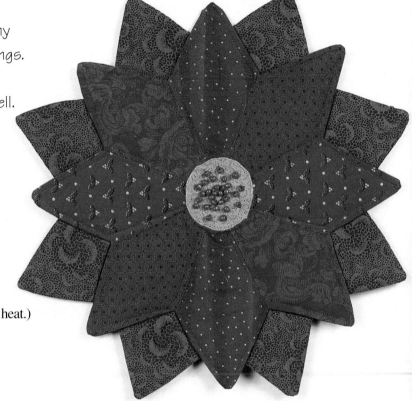

Instructions
Step 1. Cut leaf and petals as directed on patterns.

Step 2. Trace flower center on paper side of fusible transfer web. Cut around shape leaving roughly ½" margin. Fuse to gold fabric following manufacturer's directions. Cut out on traced lines.

Step 3. Pin two leaf pieces right sides together, then pin to batting and cut out around leaf shape. Sew layers together with a ¼" seam allowance, leaving a 2" opening for turning. Turn, press and close opening with hand stitches.

Step 4. Pin flower petal pieces together, alternating various red prints. Stitch together on the adjoining side edges only. Press seams as you go.

Step 5. Fuse prepared flower center to center of flower. Machine-appliqué around center with gold thread. Sew 24–30 red beads randomly on flower center.

Step 6. Place completed flower unit on red fabric and pin in place. Use unit as a pattern to cut flower backing. With fabric pieces right sides together, pin on top of batting and cut out. Sew layers with ¼" seam allowance, leaving a 2" opening for turning. Turn, press and close opening with hand stitches.

Step 7. Place flower on top of leaf section so leaf points are centered between flower petal points. Pin together. Through all layers, stitch in the ditch around the individual petals and along the points and side seams. ✼

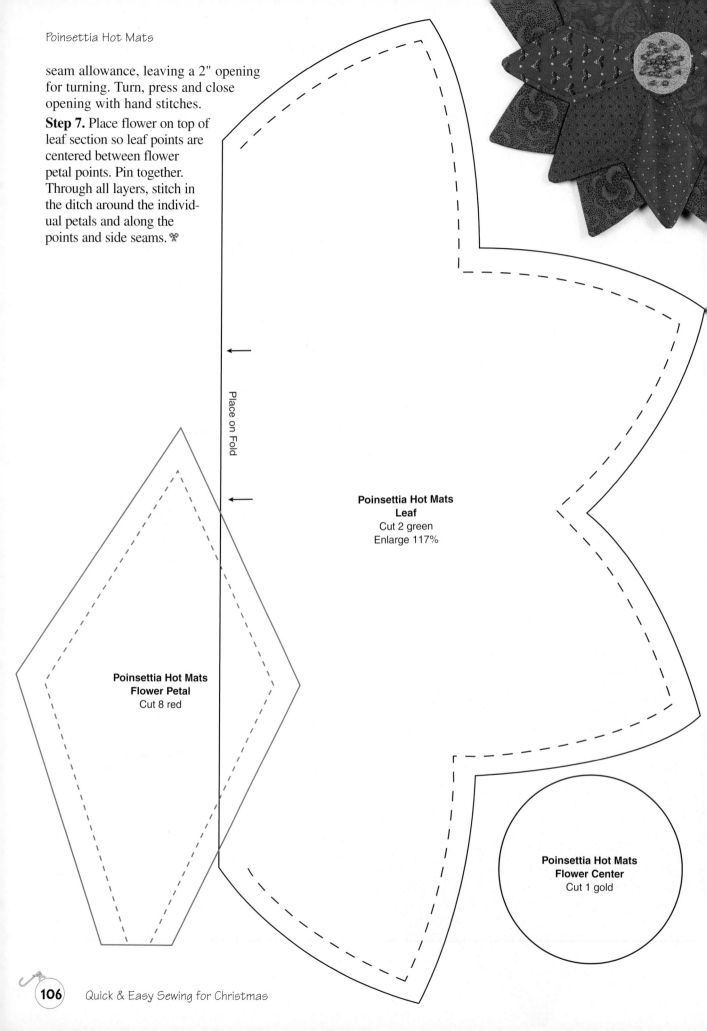

Place on Fold

**Poinsettia Hot Mats
Leaf**
Cut 2 green
Enlarge 117%

**Poinsettia Hot Mats
Flower Petal**
Cut 8 red

**Poinsettia Hot Mats
Flower Center**
Cut 1 gold

WINTER SILHOUETTES

By Karen Mead

This small-scale set would be perfect to brighten a dorm room or nursing home room. Bring Christmas to someone's home away from home.

Project Specifications

Skill Level: Beginner
Wall Hanging Size: 14" x 14"
Square Pillow Size: 12" x 12"
Small Pillow Size: 6" x 9"

Materials

Note: Materials are for four-piece set.

- ½ yard red-and-green plaid
- ¾ yard red solid to match plaid
- 3 squares green felt
- Polyester fiberfill
- 14 (½"–¾") off-white buttons
- ⅓ yard fusible transfer web
- Off-white 6-strand embroidery floss
- Air-soluble marker
- 15" (¼"-diameter) dowel rod
- 20" off-white cord
- Craft glue
- Basic sewing supplies and tools

Instructions

WALL HANGING

Note: Use ½" seam allowances throughout.

Step 1. From red solid fabric cut one piece each 15" x 15", 8" x 15" and 3" x 15". From red-and-green plaid cut one piece 8" x 15".

Step 2. Trace trees on paper side of fusible transfer web as directed on patterns. Cut out leaving roughly ½" margin around traced lines. Following manufacturer's directions, fuse to green felt. Cut out on traced lines.

Step 3. Right sides together, sew the red-and-green plaid and red solid 8" x 15" pieces together on the long sides for wall hanging front. Press seam open.

Step 4. Center the largest tree on the piece, plaid at the top; fuse.

Step 5. With air-soluble marker measure and mark 2¾"

and 4¼" in from each side on seam line. Drawing from seam allowance to seam allowance make an X that crosses marks. Referring to photo, with two strands of off-white embroidery floss, stitch the X's and sew a button to the top of the tree.

Step 6. Turn under 1" on each end of the 3" x 15" red solid rod pocket piece; press. Turn under one long edge ½"; press. Center and align other long edge with top of 15" x 15" backing piece and pin. Topstitch along fold line of lower edge through backing as shown in Fig. 1.

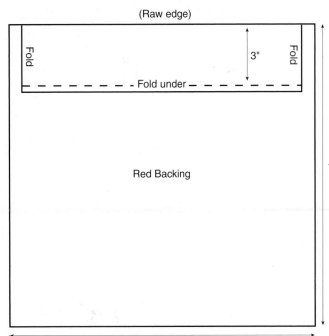

(Raw edge)

Fold

3"

Fold

– – – Fold under – – – – –

Red Backing

15"

15"

Fig. 1
Place and stitch rod pocket as shown.

Step 7. Place right sides of front and back pieces together, rod pocket at the top and tree upright. Stitch around perimeter, leaving 5" opening for turning. Clip corners and turn. Close opening with hand stitches; press.

Step 8. Sew buttons to four corners as shown in photo.

Step 9. Slip dowel rod into rod pocket on back of wall hanging. Tie 20" off-white cord around the rod about ½" from each end and glue in place. Glue a button to each end of dowel to finish.

SQUARE PILLOW

Step 1. From red solid fabric cut one piece each 13" x

13" and 7" x 13". From red-and-green plaid cut one piece 7" x 13".

Step 2. Right sides together, stitch the two 7" x 13" pieces together along one long edge. Press seam open. Center and fuse medium-size tree to piece, plaid at the bottom.

Step 3. With air-soluble marker, measure and mark 3" in from each side on seam line. Referring to photo and Step 5 of Wall Hanging, mark and stitch X's. Sew a button on each side of X's. Sew a button to the top of the tree.

Step 4. Place pillow front and red solid 13" x 13" square right sides together. Stitch around perimeter, leaving a 5" opening for turning. Clip corners and turn right side out. Press and stuff with polyester fiberfill. Close opening with hand stitches.

SMALL TWO-COLOR PILLOW

Step 1. From red solid fabric cut one piece each 7" x 10" and 4" x 7". From red-and-green plaid cut one piece 7" x 7".

Step 2. Right sides together, sew the 4" x 7" red solid and the red-and-green plaid piece together on 7" side. Press seam open.

Step 3. Center and fuse one small tree to piece, plaid at the bottom. Sew a button to the tree top.

Step 4. Place pillow front and 7" x 10" red solid piece right sides together. Stitch around perimeter, leaving a 4" opening for turning. Clip corners and turn right side out. Press and stuff lightly with polyester fiberfill. Close opening with hand stitches.

SMALL RED PILLOW

Step 1. From red solid fabric cut two pieces 7" x 10". Center and fuse one small tree to one red piece. Stitch button to top of tree.

Step 2. Place pillow top and second red solid piece right sides together. Stitch and finish as in Step 4, Small Two-Color Pillow. ❦

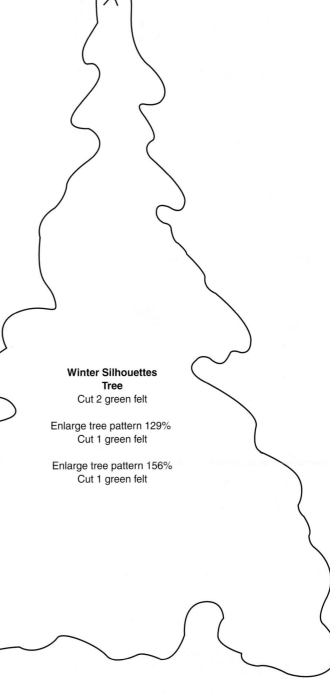

Winter Silhouettes Tree
Cut 2 green felt

Enlarge tree pattern 129%
Cut 1 green felt

Enlarge tree pattern 156%
Cut 1 green felt

MOONLIGHT TREES CENTERPIECE

By Phyllis M. Dobbs

Make this cheery little topper for an end table, the coffee table or any dresser or chest in your house to lend a little Christmas joy. It is remarkably quick and easy.

Project Specifications
Skill Level: Beginner
Centerpiece Size: 13" x 18"

Materials
- Green felt 13" x 18"
- Ivory felt 10½" x 15½"
- Scraps of yellow felt
- 12 assorted red buttons
- Scraps of fusible transfer web
- Green, yellow and red all-purpose thread
- Air-soluble marker
- Basic sewing supplies and tools

Instructions
Step 1. Trace and cut out tree patterns. Referring to photo, place patterns on ivory felt and trace around shapes with air-soluble marker. Carefully cut out and remove tree shapes from ivory piece.

Step 2. Trace five stars and one moon on paper side of fusible transfer web. Cut out leaving roughly ½" margin around shapes. Following manufacturer's directions, fuse to yellow felt and cut out on traced lines. Referring to photo for placement, arrange on ivory felt and fuse in place. With yellow thread, topstitch around edges of stars and moon.

Step 3. Pin ivory piece to green felt background piece. Pin around edges and around trees. Stitch with green thread around edges of trees and then around outside edge of ivory felt.

Step 4. Sew red buttons to treetops and down center of each tree, referring to photo for placement. ❧

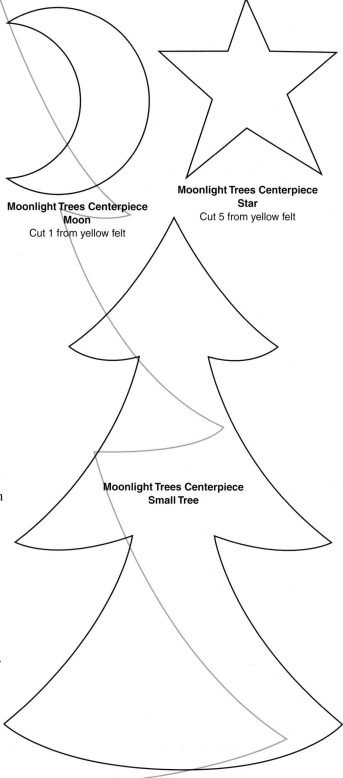

Moonlight Trees Centerpiece Moon
Cut 1 from yellow felt

Moonlight Trees Centerpiece Star
Cut 5 from yellow felt

Moonlight Trees Centerpiece Small Tree

Moonlight Trees Centerpiece Large Tree

Cutwork Snowflakes Mantel Scarf

Continued from page 91

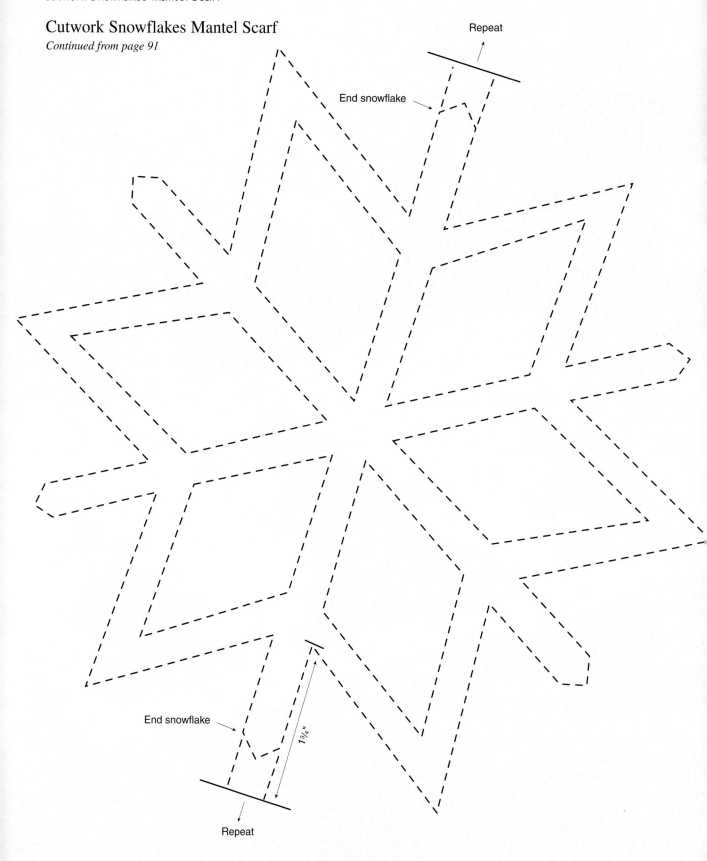

Repeat

End snowflake

End snowflake

1 3/4"

Repeat

Cutwork Snowflake Mantel Scarf
Snowflake Pattern

Gingerbread Grins Pillow

Continued from page 89

**Gingerbread Grins
Scarf**
Cut 1 green felt

**Gingerbread Grins
Gingerbread Man**
Cut 1 tan felt

SANTA'S WORKSHOP

No Christmas home is complete without Santas and snowmen and all sorts of little Christmas characters.

In these pages you'll find little elves, teddy bears, and all sorts of Santas to sit on shelves or in any corner that needs a touch of Christmas. A toasty warm snowman will melt your heart with holiday charm. And our holiday windsocks will add cheer to the most blustery of winter days!

You'll find yourself smiling with glee as you stitch this appealing assortment of holiday figures!

FLYING SANTA WIND SOCK

By Lee Lindeman

What fun to greet the mailman, neighborhood children and anyone who passes your home with a frisky wind-borne Santa of your own creation!

Project Specifications
Skill Level: Beginner
Wind Sock Size: Approximately 12" x 31"

Materials
- 1 yard red nylon ripstop
- ½ yard white nylon ripstop
- ¼ yard black nylon ripstop
- ¼ yard pink nylon ripstop
- Scrap of gold fabric for belt buckle
- 8" metal ring
- All-purpose threads to match fabrics
- 2 yards ⅛"-wide red satin ribbon for hanger
- Small amount of polyester fiberfill
- 2 (⅝") black buttons
- Large tapestry needle
- Basic sewing supplies and tools

Instructions
Step 1. For the main portion of the wind sock, cut one strip each from red nylon 4¼" x 26" and 13" x 26". From white nylon cut one strip 6½" x 26". Sew the white strip between the two red strips on long edges with a ¼" seam allowance.

Step 2. Turn under the long raw edge of the 13" strip ¼" and then ¾" and hem. Turn ¼" under on long raw edge of the 4¼" strip and sew.

Step 3. Draw around patterns on doubled pieces of nylon (except nose and hat pompom circles). Sew on drawn lines, leaving openings for turning each piece right side out. Trim to ¼" seam allowance, turn and press with cool iron. Repeat with each pattern part.

Step 4. From red nylon cut two legs 7" x 8½". From white nylon cut two leg cuffs 2¼" x 7" and two sleeve cuffs 6¼" x 4¼".

Step 5. Right sides together, fold legs in half lengthwise and stitch long raw edges and across one short end with ¼" seam allowance. Turn right side out and press with cool iron.

Step 6. Fold sleeve and leg cuffs in half lengthwise. Press fold with cool iron. Press long raw edges under ¼". Bring right sides of short ends together and stitch with ¼" seam allowance.

Step 7. Turn open end of sleeves under ¼" and press with cool iron. Insert mitten into end of each sleeve; topstitch. Insert each sleeve in a cuff so mitten extends from cuff. Topstitch in place at upper edge, leaving lower folded edge free.

Step 8. Turn under ¼" at open boot top; press. Insert each leg into a boot; topstitch. Insert each leg in a cuff so boot extends from cuff. Topstitch in place at upper edge, leaving lower folded edge free.

Step 9. Close opening in mustache with hand stitches. Referring to photo, position mustache and black buttons for eyes. Sew in place. Cut one red nose circle and run an unknotted basting stitch around the outside edge. Place a little polyester fiberfill in the center and pull up the two thread ends to enclose. Tie to secure. Sew in place on face.

Step 10. From black nylon cut one strip 4" x 26" for belt. Press under ¼" on each long side. Position 6" down from top of wide red body strip. Topstitch in place. Topstitch gold belt buckle to center front.

Step 11. Center face on center white strip; pin in place. Position beard over lower face; topstitch inner curve only, sewing both face and beard to white strip. Sew hair across top of face on straight edge only.

Step 12. Position sleeves on body as shown in Fig. 1. Sew across shoulder. Fold sleeves back down over seam. Sew legs to wrong side of center front, positioned as shown in Fig. 1. Be sure you have right and left mittens and boots.

Step 13. From white nylon cut two strips 4½" x 26". Fold in half lengthwise; press. Fold under and press ¼" on each long edge. Position one folded strip on ¾" seam at bottom of suit. Pin and topstitch for suit bottom cuff. Position second folded strip on white/red seam between face and hat; pin and topstitch. Folded edge will hang free.

Step 14. Bring right sides of center back together. Stitch and turn right side out.

Step 15. Place metal ring on inside at top. Turn top edge down over ring and sew in place with hand stitches.

Step 16. Cut ribbon in three equal parts. Thread one ribbon through eye of tapestry needle. Carefully sew through top hem under wire from inside to outside. Pull

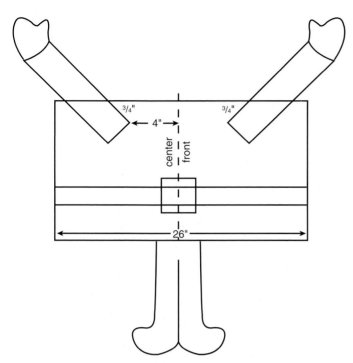

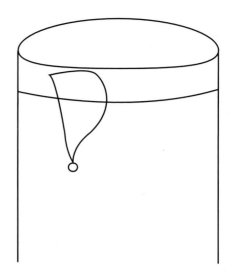

Fig. 1
Position sleeves and legs on body
as shown.

Fig. 2
Sew hat on wrong side as shown.

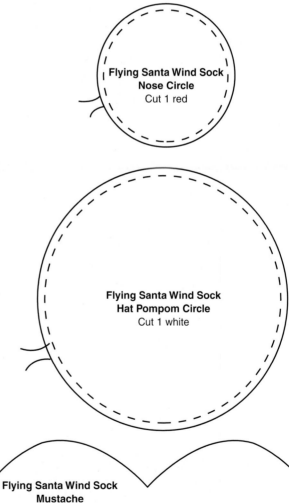

Flying Santa Wind Sock
Nose Circle
Cut 1 red

Flying Santa Wind Sock
Hat Pompom Circle
Cut 1 white

through leaving ½" on the inside to sew to the outside length of ribbon, securing to ring. Repeat with two more ribbons spaced evenly around the top. Tie top ends together and decorate with a bow below the knot.

Step 17. From white nylon cut one hat pompom circle and run an unknotted basting stitch around the outside edge. Place a little polyester fiberfill in the center and pull up the two thread ends to enclose. Tie to secure. Sew in place on end of hat.

Step 18. Fold under and press ¼" on open end of hat; topstitch. With hand stitches sew to wrong side of hat, pompom pointing down as shown in Fig. 2. When sewn in place, flip up and over ring to hang free on outside. ❅

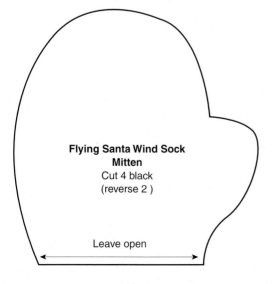

Flying Santa Wind Sock
Mitten
Cut 4 black
(reverse 2)

Leave open

Flying Santa Wind Sock
Mustache
Cut 2 white
(reverse 1)

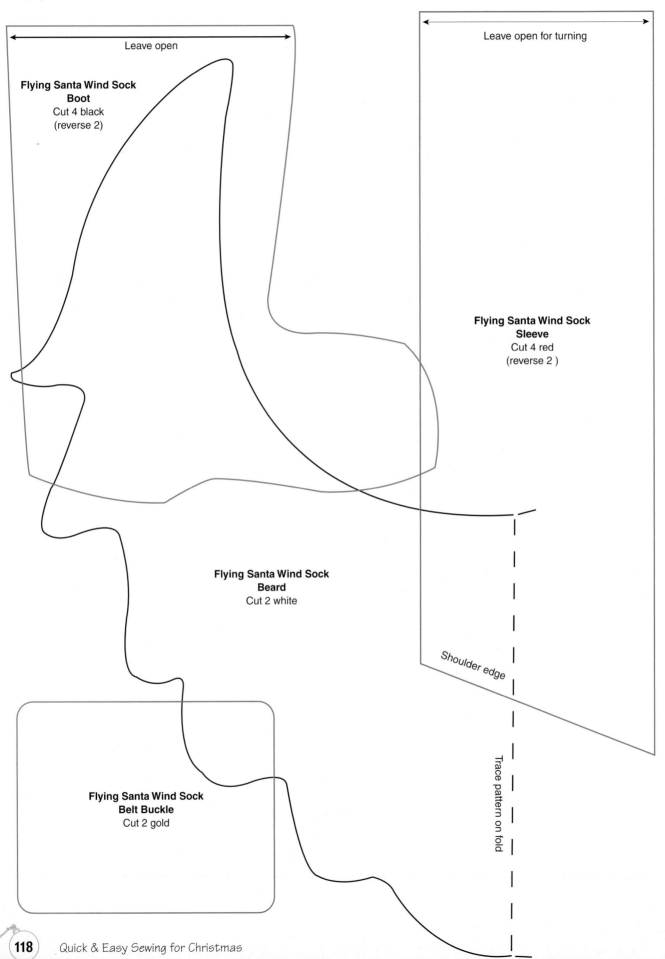

Leave open

**Flying Santa Wind Sock
Boot**
Cut 4 black
(reverse 2)

Leave open for turning

**Flying Santa Wind Sock
Sleeve**
Cut 4 red
(reverse 2)

**Flying Santa Wind Sock
Beard**
Cut 2 white

Shoulder edge

Trace pattern on fold

**Flying Santa Wind Sock
Belt Buckle**
Cut 2 gold

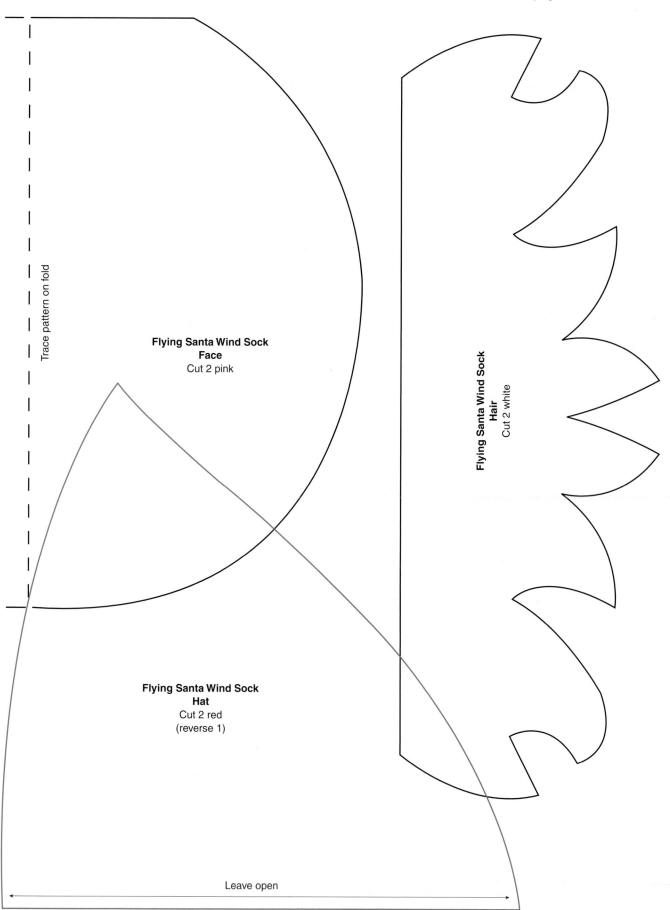

Trace pattern on fold

Flying Santa Wind Sock
Face
Cut 2 pink

Flying Santa Wind Sock
Hair
Cut 2 white

Flying Santa Wind Sock
Hat
Cut 2 red
(reverse 1)

Leave open

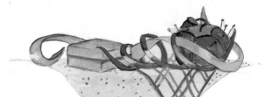

BLUSTERY SNOWMAN WIND SOCK

By Lee Lindeman

You can hang this wind sock when you anticipate the first snowflake; he'll cheer you right through Christmas and until the spring thaw.

Project Specifications
Skill Level: Beginner
Wind Sock Size: Approximately 12" x 39"

Materials
- ¾ yard light blue nylon ripstop
- 1 yard white nylon ripstop
- Scraps of red, orange, black and green nylon ripstop
- 8" metal ring
- All-purpose threads to match fabrics
- 2 yards ¼"-wide white satin ribbon
- 2 (⅝") black buttons for eyes
- 3 (1") black buttons for body buttons
- 1 (⅜") red button for holly
- Large tapestry needle
- White marking pencil
- Basic sewing supplies and tools

Instructions
Step 1. From light blue nylon cut a background piece 25" x 23". With a cool iron press under one long edge ¼" and then ¾". Stitch to hem. Turn over other long edge (top) ¼" and sew.

Step 2. Trace patterns and place appliqué pieces on doubled fabrics as directed on templates. Trace around each and stitch through both pieces of fabric on drawn lines, leaving an opening for turning. Cut out leaving ¼" seam allowance. Turn right side out and press with cool iron.

Step 3. Trace mouth on face from pattern. Machine-stitch with narrow zigzag and black thread. Sew small black buttons in place for eyes. Stitch stem-end of carrot in place, leaving carrot free. Sew large black buttons on body.

Step 4. From white nylon cut four strips 4¾" x 25". Place two strips right sides together and draw a free-form line for snow as shown in Fig. 1. Place the other two strips right sides together and draw a shape similar

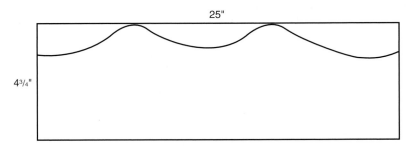

Fig. 1
Draw free-form line as shown.

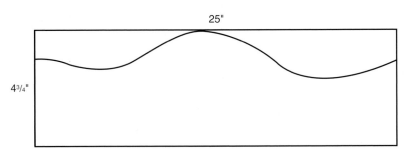

Fig. 2
Draw free-form line as shown.

to Fig. 2. Pin each pair of strips together and stitch each pair on the drawn line. Turn right side out and press. Turn under ¼" on straight edges and press.

Step 5. Align lower pressed folds of Fig. 1 strip with lower edge of blue background strip. Topstitch along the curved edge.

Step 6. Referring to photo, arrange appliqué pieces on background. Pin and then baste in place. Topstitch in place leaving arms and scarf ends free. Leave bottom of tree open for a more dimensional look.

Step 7. Sew holly leaves and red button to hat with hand stitches.

Step 8. Align lower pressed folds of Fig. 2 strip with lower edge of blue background strip. Topstitch along the curved edge.

Step 9. From white nylon cut 15 wind-tails 2½" x 19". Turn a scant ¼" under twice on two long sides and one short end. Stitch to hem. Insert between blue background and turned-under edges of snow layers. Pin side-by-side evenly along lower edge, leaving a scant ½" at each side for seam allowance. Baste and then topstitch through all layers.

Step 10. Right sides facing, bring back edges together and stitch. Turn right side out.

Step 11. Place metal ring on inside at top. Turn top edge over metal ring and sew with hand stitches.

Step 12. Cut ribbon in three equal parts. Thread one ribbon through eye of tapestry needle. Carefully sew through top hem under wire from inside to outside. Pull through leaving ½" on the inside to sew to the outside length of ribbon, securing to ring. Repeat with two more ribbons spaced evenly around the top. Tie top ends together and decorate with a bow below the knot. ❅

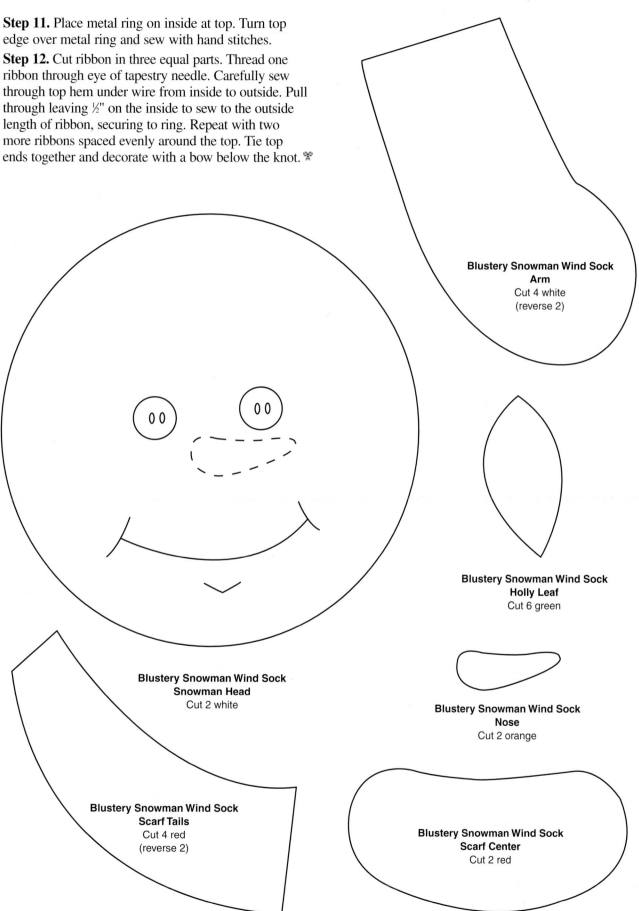

**Blustery Snowman Wind Sock
Arm**
Cut 4 white
(reverse 2)

**Blustery Snowman Wind Sock
Holly Leaf**
Cut 6 green

**Blustery Snowman Wind Sock
Snowman Head**
Cut 2 white

**Blustery Snowman Wind Sock
Nose**
Cut 2 orange

**Blustery Snowman Wind Sock
Scarf Tails**
Cut 4 red
(reverse 2)

**Blustery Snowman Wind Sock
Scarf Center**
Cut 2 red

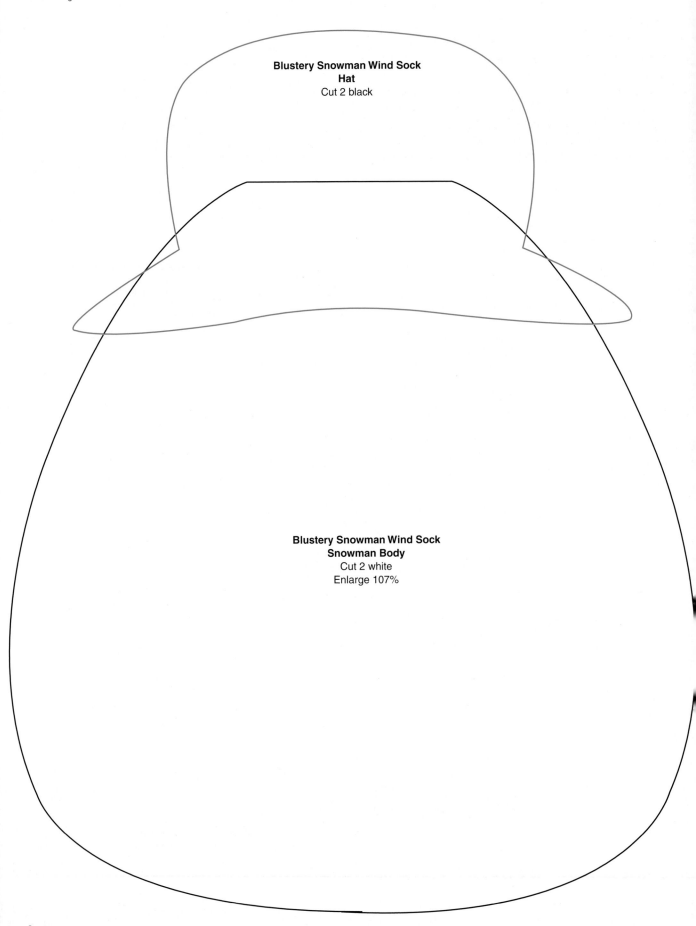

Blustery Snowman Wind Sock
Hat
Cut 2 black

Blustery Snowman Wind Sock
Snowman Body
Cut 2 white
Enlarge 107%

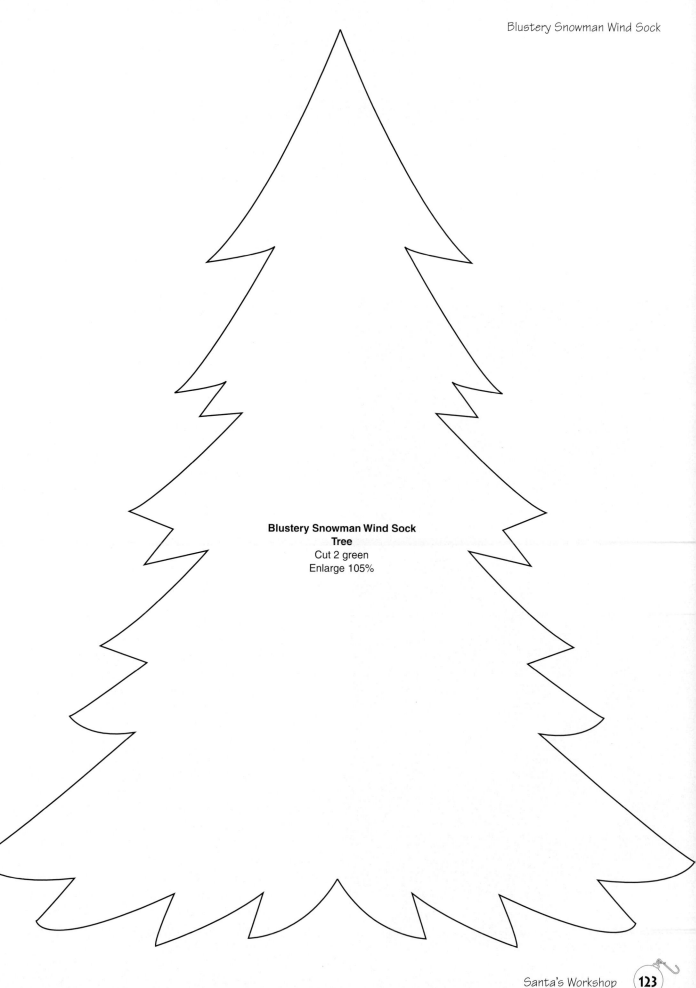

Blustery Snowman Wind Sock
Tree
Cut 2 green
Enlarge 105%

FOLK SANTA DOLL

By Nancy Brenan Daniel

This Santa is charmingly pieced from scraps of old cutter quilts. Add a few buttons, a batting beard and whimsical expression and you've got a heart stealer for sure!

Project Specifications
Skill Level: Beginner
Santa Size: Approximately 14" tall

Materials
- ¼ yard cutter-quilt remnant or recycled wool
- 1" x 45" strip brown plush felt
- 4" x 8" flesh-tone fabric for head
- 6" x 8" red print fabric for arms
- 3" x 12" cotton batting for beard and hair
- 3" x 3" red felt for heart
- 5" x 5" recycled wool, cutter-quilt remnant or felt for bag
- 1 scrap each 5" x 5" and 5" x 10" for bag lining
- 1 ½" x 12" strip for bag strap
- 12 oz. polyester fiberfill
- ½ cup pellets
- Rose and black 6-strand embroidery floss
- 1 (⅞") wooden heart button
- 7 buttons of various sizes and colors for embellishment
- ¼" pink pompom for nose
- Basic sewing supplies and tools

Instructions
Step 1. Cut coat, sleeves and hat as directed on templates.

Step 2. Right sides together, sew around coat pieces leaving opening as shown on template. Match side and bottom seams at each side and sew across as shown in Fig. 1 to create a flat box bottom. Turn right side out. Pour pellets into body and then stuff firmly with polyester fiberfill. Close opening with hand stitches.

Step 3. Right sides together, sew hat and sleeves, leaving openings at bottom. Turn right side out.

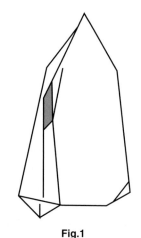

Fig.1
Match side and bottom seams and sew across as shown.

Step 4. Trace around arm pattern piece twice on right-sides-together doubled red print. Sew around arms on the traced line leaving opening as shown. Cut out leaving ⅛" seam allowance. Turn right side out and stuff. Close opening with hand stitches.

Step 5. Push arms into sleeves allowing hand to extend from sleeve opening.

Step 6. Trace around head pattern piece on doubled flesh-tone fabric. Sew around head on traced line, leaving opening as shown. Cut out leaving ⅛" seam allowance. Turn right side out and stuff. Close opening with hand stitches.

Step 7. With black embroidery floss embroider eyes and with rose floss stitch mouth. Sew or glue pompom in place for nose.

Step 8. Make ¾" clips in batting strip approximately ¼" apart on each side of strip as shown in Fig. 2. Fold strip in half lengthwise and sew by hand around Santa's face and back of lower head as shown in Fig. 3.

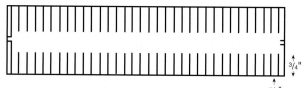

Fig. 2
Clip batting strip for beard as shown.

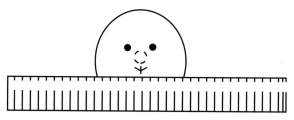

Fig. 3
Sew folded beard to lower face and
back of head.

Step 9. Measure around end of each sleeve for cuff. Cut brown plush felt to fit; with 6 strands of black embroidery floss, sew cuff to sleeve crudely. Sew a button where ends meet to hold in place.

Step 10. Measure around hat opening and cut brown plush felt to fit. Finish as for sleeve.

Step 11. Measure down coat front and around coat bottom. Cut brown plush felt strips to fit. Finish as for sleeve, referring to photo for button placement.

Step 12. From red felt trace and cut heart. Sew to chest area of coat with 6 strands of black embroidery floss. Add wooden heart button.

Step 13. Sew head to body. Attach arms to body with buttons so they are movable. Sew hat to head.

Step 14. Fold bag strap in half lengthwise and sew along edge. Turn right side out; press. Align raw ends of strap near outer edges of right side of bag fabric square. Place 5" x 5" lining square face down on top and stitch across edge, catching ends of strap in seam. Place 5" x 10" lining piece facing bag and stitch around three sides, leaving top open. Turn right side

out and stuff lining down into bag. Place over shoulder as shown in photo. ❈

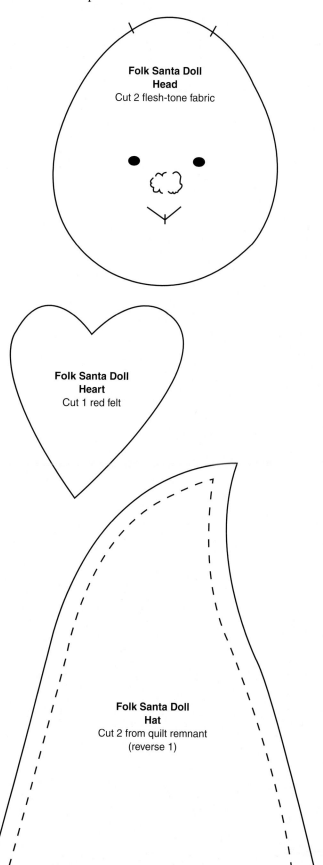

Folk Santa Doll
Head
Cut 2 flesh-tone fabric

Folk Santa Doll
Heart
Cut 1 red felt

Folk Santa Doll
Hat
Cut 2 from quilt remnant
(reverse 1)

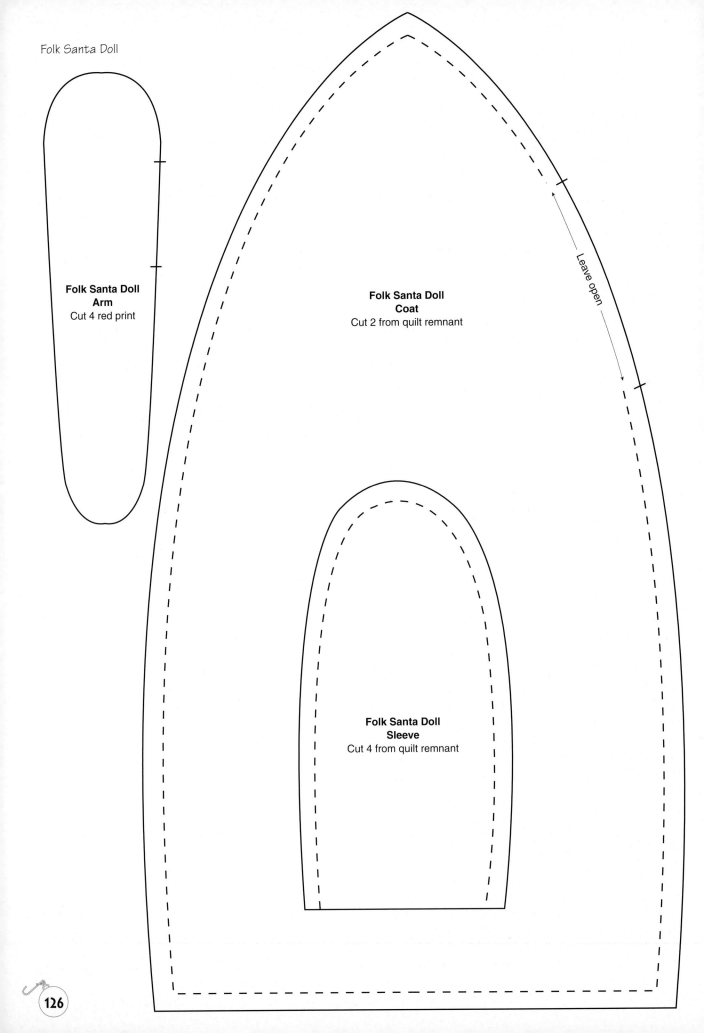

**Folk Santa Doll
Arm**
Cut 4 red print

**Folk Santa Doll
Coat**
Cut 2 from quilt remnant

Leave open

**Folk Santa Doll
Sleeve**
Cut 4 from quilt remnant

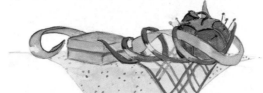

L'IL BEAR HUGS TEDDY BEAR

By Julie DeGroat

Everyone needs a cute little bear to sit on the Christmas tree, peek out of a basket or give to a special child. Make this bear in about an hour. He will look adorable done in fake fur, Christmas fabric or rich velvet.

Project Specifications
Skill Level: Beginner
Teddy Bear Size: Approximately 7" x 9"

Materials
- 20" x 15" fake fur
- 5" x 5" contrasting fabric for ear lining
- 2 post-type lock-on animal eyes (or buttons)
- 1 post-type lock-on animal nose (or button)
- Red 6-strand embroidery floss
- Polyester fiberfill
- ½ yard ⅝"-wide ribbon
- Basic sewing supplies and tools

Instructions
Step 1. Cut fabrics as directed on templates.

Step 2. Place ear lining pieces right sides together with fur ears. Sew around the top curve with a ¼" seam. Leave bottom open.

Step 3. Turn ears right side out and pin to the right side of the body front, ear lining facing body fur and raw edges aligned. Use the markings on the pattern as a placement guide.

Step 4. Pin body front to body back, right sides together. The previously pinned ears will be sandwiched between the body front and body back. Sew around body, leaving opening for stuffing.

Step 5. Turn right side out, stuff with polyester fiberfill and close opening with hand stitches.

Step 6. Sew the two side darts in the face piece. Fur side facing you, attach the eyes and nose, referring to the pattern piece for placement.

Step 7. Pin the completed face to the front of the bear's head. Be sure it is the front by checking the ear linings. Stitch tightly ¾ of the way around with hand stitches. If you are using fabric, you will need to roll a slight hem under as you sew. Fur does not

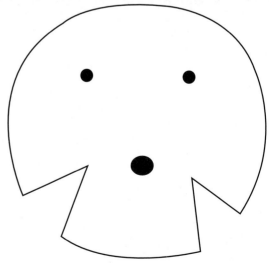

**L'il Bear Hugs
Teddy Bear Face**
Cut 1 fake fur

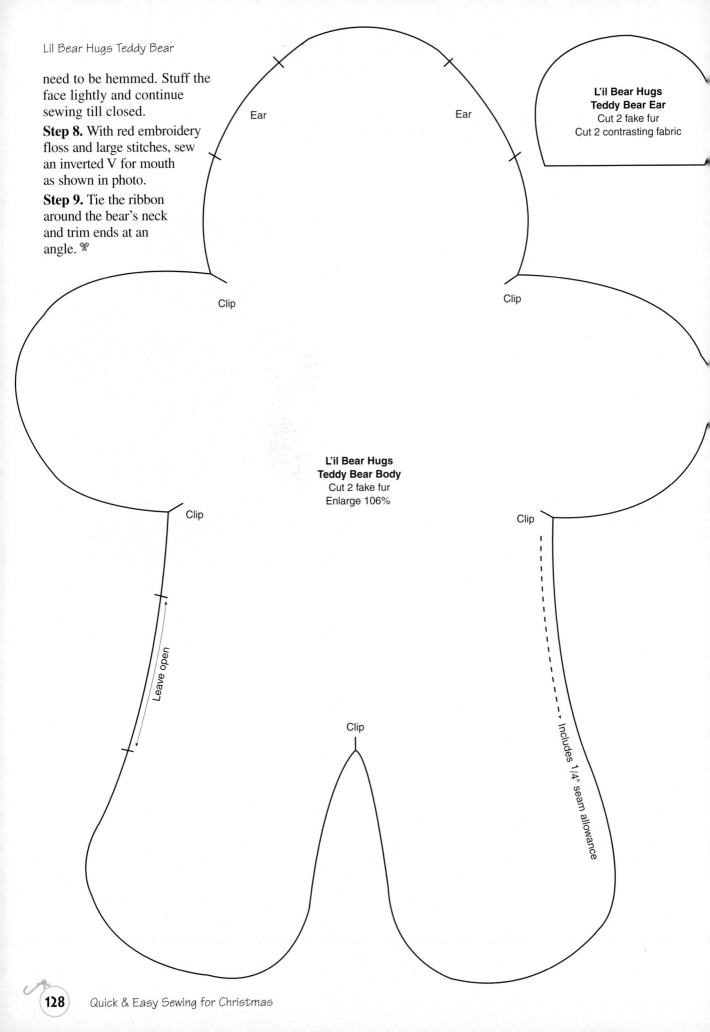

Lil Bear Hugs Teddy Bear

need to be hemmed. Stuff the face lightly and continue sewing till closed.

Step 8. With red embroidery floss and large stitches, sew an inverted V for mouth as shown in photo.

Step 9. Tie the ribbon around the bear's neck and trim ends at an angle. ✻

Ear

Ear

L'il Bear Hugs Teddy Bear Ear
Cut 2 fake fur
Cut 2 contrasting fabric

Clip

Clip

Clip

Clip

L'il Bear Hugs Teddy Bear Body
Cut 2 fake fur
Enlarge 106%

Leave open

Clip

Includes 1/4" seam allowance

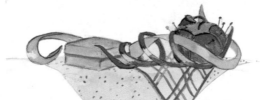

WEE SANTA SHELF SITTER

By Phyllis M. Dobbs

You'll think of dozens of places to tuck this little guy—tied to packages, peeking out of a bag of home-baked goodies or even pinned to your lapel. Be sure to whip up enough!

Project Specifications
Skill Level: Beginner
Shelf Sitter Size: Approximately 10" x 2½"

Materials
- Scraps of red fabric
- Scraps of light tan fabric
- Scraps of red felt
- Scrap of green felt
- Polyester fiberfill
- 7" (⅜"-wide) green satin ribbon
- ⅝" red star-shaped sew-on rhinestone
- ½" green star button
- 2 silver-lined blue glass rochaille beads
- Mohair fuzzy doll hair
- Basic sewing supplies and tools

Instructions
Step 1. Cut fabrics as directed on templates. From light tan fabric cut two strips 1¾" x 9½" for legs and two strips 1¾" x 5½" for arms.

Step 2. To one head piece, sew blue glass rochaille beads in place for eyes. Right sides together, pin head front to head back and sew with ¼" seam allowance. Leave bottom of neck open. Trim close to seam, turn and press.

Step 3. Fold each arm and leg piece lengthwise, right sides together. Stitch long edge and across one end with ¼" seam. Trim seams, turn and press.

Step 4. Referring to photo, position arms and legs on right side of one body piece, raw edges aligned. Pin right side of other body piece in place, sandwiching arms and legs inside. Stitch around edges, being careful to include only seam allowance of arms and legs in seam. Leave an opening for turning. Trim seams, turn and press.

Step 5. Tie a single knot in each leg to form knee and in each arm to form elbow.

Step 6. Stitch fuzzy doll hair around head and across face under eyes. Trim ends even.

Step 7. Wrap green ⅜"-wide satin ribbon around body, overlapping in back. Fold end under and stitch ribbon to doll back. Sew red star-shaped sew-on rhinestone to front of ribbon belt.

Step 8. Pin two pieces of cap together and stitch around curve close to edge, leaving bottom open. Place over top of head and stitch in place. Sew green star button to top right of cap.

Step 9. Pin two pieces of boot together and stitch around curves close to edge, leaving top open. Repeat for two boots. Place ends of legs in boots and hand-stitch across top.

Step 10. Tack green stocking to end of one arm. ❋

Wee Santa Shelf Sitter
Cap
Cut 2 red felt

Wee Santa Shelf Sitter
Head
Cut 2 light tan

Wee Santa Shelf Sitter
Boot
Cut 4 red felt

Wee Santa Shelf Sitter
Body
Cut 2 red

Wee Santa Shelf Sitter
Stocking
Cut 1 green felt

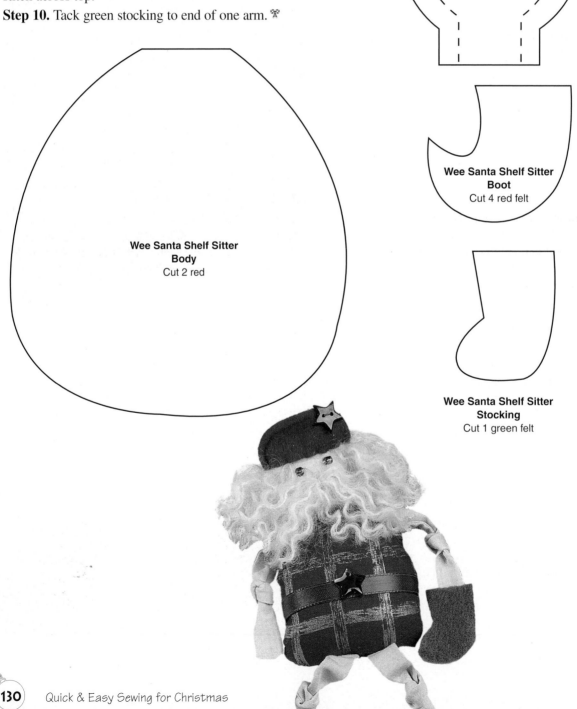

CHRISTMAS PUPPETS

By Connie Matricardi

Just imagine the stories that might be told by these three familiar characters. A great way to entertain the little ones when pre-Christmas excitement gets high!

Project Specifications
Skill Level: Beginner
Puppet Size: Approximately 9" x 11"

Materials
Note: Materials and instructions are for the set of three.

- 2 rectangles 9" x 12" each of red and tan felt
- 3 rectangles 9" x 12" white felt
- Scraps of apple green, black, orange, pink and flesh-tone felt
- 1 rectangle 9" x 12" white plush felt
- All-purpose threads to match felt
- 1 package white medium rickrack
- 3 (⅝") black shank buttons for Santa
- 3 (¾") black buttons for snowman
- 3 (¾") red buttons for gingerbread man
- 1 (1") white pompom for Santa hat
- 1 (7mm) pink pompom for Santa nose
- 2 (⅜") black pompoms for snowman eyes
- 3 (5mm) red pompoms for holly berries
- 4 (8mm) round black beads for eyes
- 8" (⅝"-wide) red-and-white striped ribbon
- 6" x 6" Craft-Bond, Crisp Iron-on backing material from Pellon
- Craft glue
- Air-soluble marker
- Powdered cosmetic blush
- Cotton swab
- Basic sewing supplies and tools

Instructions

SANTA

Step 1. Cut felt pieces as directed on patterns.

Step 2. Pin white felt coat trim to Santa front for lining. Place white plush trim on top of white felt. Topstitch through all layers.

Step 3. Sew three ⅝" black shank buttons to coat trim.

Step 4. Pin Santa front to Santa back. Pin a mitten to the end of each arm (thumbs up). Sew around perimeter, leaving bottom open.

Step 5. Sew white plush beard layer to white felt layer around outer edge. Referring to photo for placement, sew flesh-tone face to beard layers. Sew 8mm black beads in place for eyes. With cosmetic blush and cotton swab, lightly brush round cheeks on Santa face. Glue mouth, mustache, pompom nose and eyebrows in place.

Step 6. Position and glue Santa head to puppet front. Glue white pompom to hat. Glue white plush felt cuffs to Santa arms.

SNOWMAN

Step 1. Cut felt pieces as directed on patterns.

Step 2. Referring to photo, glue black pompom eyes and carrot nose to snowman head. Draw smile with air-soluble marker. With black thread, machine-stitch traced line.

Step 3. Referring to photo, glue red stripes to green scarf. Trim stripes to match scarf, if necessary. Clip ends of scarf as shown on pattern for fringe. Glue scarf to snowman front, leaving fringed end free.

Step 4. Sew three ¾" black buttons to snowman front.

Step 5. Pin snowman front to snowman back. Sew around perimeter, leaving bottom open.

Step 6. Fuse Craft-Bond to hat back, following manufacturer's directions. Glue hat back to back of snowman head. Glue hat front to front of snowman head.

Step 7. Glue holly leaves and three red pompoms to hat.

GINGERBREAD MAN

Step 1. Cut felt pieces as directed on patterns.

Step 2. Sew white rickrack to perimeter of gingerbread man front.

Step 3. Sew 8mm black beads in place for eyes. Draw smile with air-soluble marker. With black thread, machine-stitch mouth. Glue pink cheeks to face.

Step 4. Cut a 6" length of red-and-white striped ribbon. Form a loop and tack at center. Cut a 1¼" length of ribbon. Wrap tightly around loop and tack at back. Referring to photo, sew bow in place by hand.

Step 5. Sew three ¾" red buttons to gingerbread man front.

Step 6. Pin gingerbread man front to gingerbread man back. Sew around perimeter, leaving bottom edge open. ❄

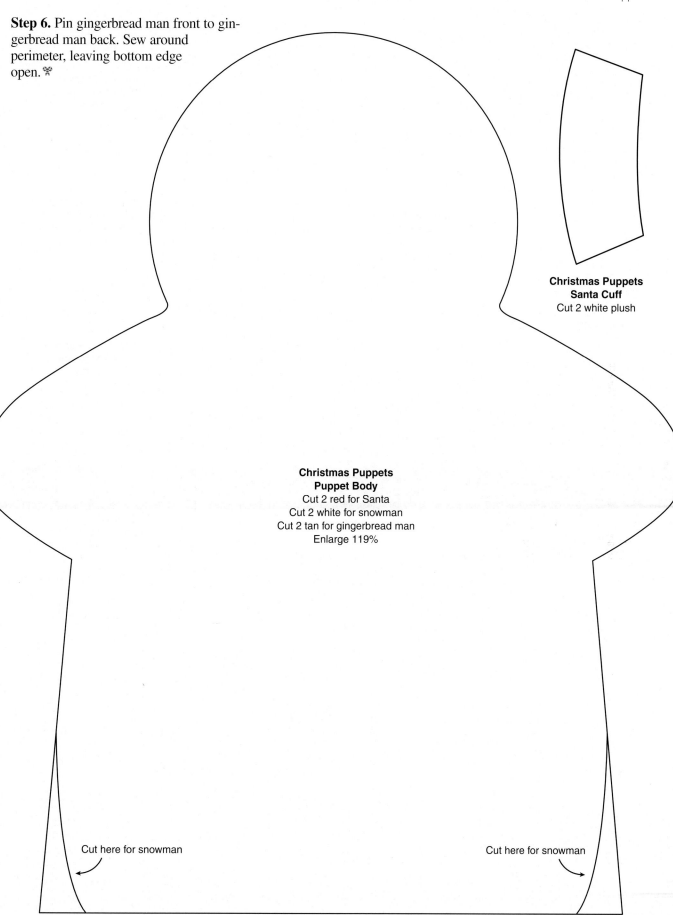

**Christmas Puppets
Santa Cuff**
Cut 2 white plush

**Christmas Puppets
Puppet Body**
Cut 2 red for Santa
Cut 2 white for snowman
Cut 2 tan for gingerbread man
Enlarge 119%

Cut here for snowman

Cut here for snowman

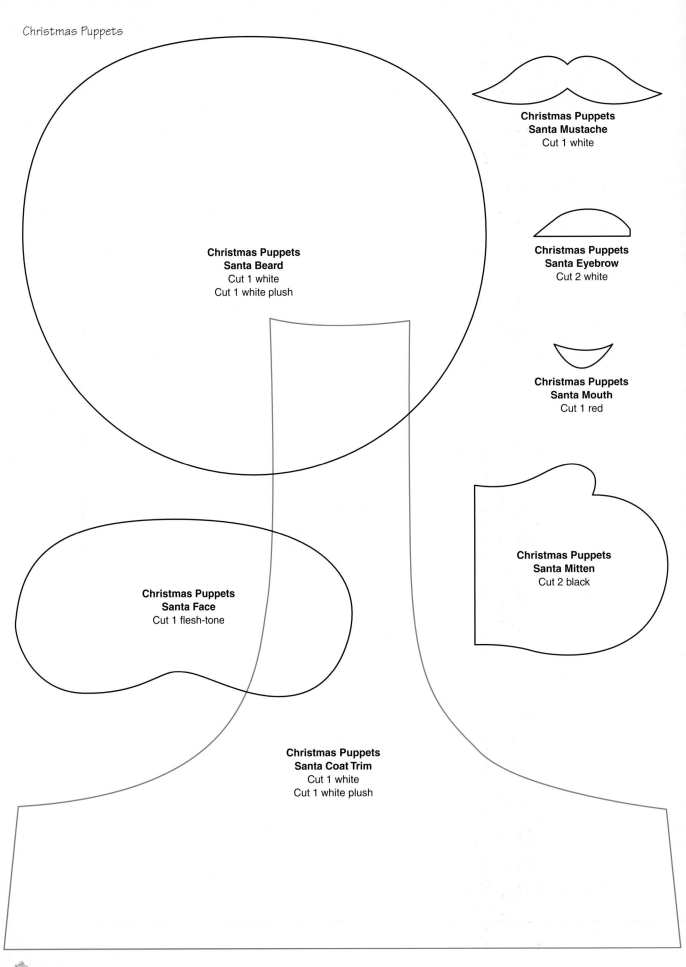

**Christmas Puppets
Santa Mustache**
Cut 1 white

**Christmas Puppets
Santa Beard**
Cut 1 white
Cut 1 white plush

**Christmas Puppets
Santa Eyebrow**
Cut 2 white

**Christmas Puppets
Santa Mouth**
Cut 1 red

**Christmas Puppets
Santa Mitten**
Cut 2 black

**Christmas Puppets
Santa Face**
Cut 1 flesh-tone

**Christmas Puppets
Santa Coat Trim**
Cut 1 white
Cut 1 white plush

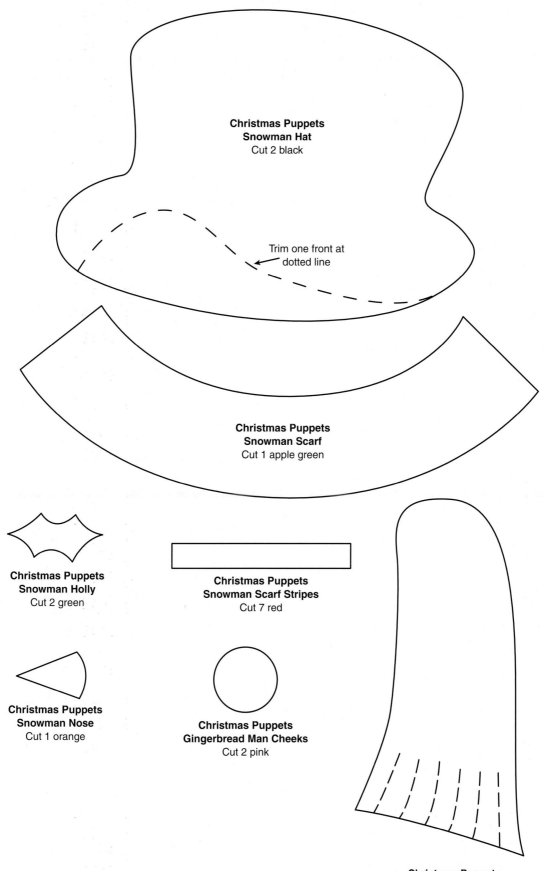

**Christmas Puppets
Snowman Hat
Cut 2 black**

Trim one front at
dotted line

**Christmas Puppets
Snowman Scarf
Cut 1 apple green**

**Christmas Puppets
Snowman Holly
Cut 2 green**

**Christmas Puppets
Snowman Scarf Stripes
Cut 7 red**

**Christmas Puppets
Snowman Nose
Cut 1 orange**

**Christmas Puppets
Gingerbread Man Cheeks
Cut 2 pink**

**Christmas Puppets
Snowman Fringed Scarf End
Cut 1 apple green**

TOASTY WARM SNOWMAN

By Julie Weaver

A warm snowman might spell trouble in real-life, but in fabric we can enjoy this contradiction all winter long.

Project Specifications
Skill Level: Beginner
Snowman Size: Approximately 6" x 12"

Materials
- ½ yard unbleached muslin
- ⅓ yard plaid Berber-type polar fleece for coat
- ½ yard solid Berber-type polar fleece for hat, coat trim and scarf
- 2 cups of weight product (plastic pebbles, silica sand, etc.)
- Red and black fine-line permanent markers
- Polyester fiberfill
- Powdered cosmetic blush
- Cotton swab
- 3 novelty buttons
- Cool temperature hot-glue gun and glue
- All-purpose threads to match fabrics
- Basic sewing supplies and tools

Instructions
Note: Patterns include ¼" seam allowance.

Step 1. Cut fabrics as directed on patterns.

Step 2. Trace facial features onto one body piece with pencil. With right sides together, sew around body, leaving open where indicated on pattern. Bring side and bottom seams together. Pull corner out to a point as shown in Fig. 1. With both seams together, stitch 1" from corner point across both seams. Repeat for second side; trim seams.

Step 3. Turn body right side out. Fill bottom with weight product. Stuff the rest of the body firmly with polyester fiberfill. Close opening with hand stitches.

Step 4. With right sides together, sew around arms leaving tops open. Stuff firmly to line indicated on pattern. Bring seams together and stitch tops. Sew or glue to snowman shoulders.

Step 5. Trace and fill in facial features with red and black permanent markers.

Step 6. From solid polar fleece cut a strip 8" x 18", with the 8" width on the stretch of the fabric. Right sides facing, fold in half lengthwise and sew the long edges. With the tube still wrong side out, turn up one open end 3½" and sew ¼" from raw edge. Tie the other end tightly about 1" from the raw edge. Turn hat right side out. Turn hemmed edge up about 2" to form a cuff. Tie other end tightly to form a ball at the end of the hat.

Step 7. From solid polar fleece cut a piece 3" x 18" for the scarf. Make 1" snips ¼" apart on each end for fringe.

Step 8. Cut up the center of coat front. From solid polar fleece cut two strips 2½" x 4" for sleeve trim. Right sides together, sew trim to end of each sleeve. Cut even with sleeve if necessary. Fold trim out.

Step 9. Right sides together, sew side, sleeve and trim seams. Turn coat right side out. Fold trim in half to inside of coat and slip-stitch in place.

Step 10. From solid polar fleece cut a strip 2½" x 19". Right sides together, sew trim to bottom of coat. Fold trim in half to the inside and slip-stitch in place. Cut trim even with coat front opening, if necessary.

Step 11. From solid polar fleece cut a strip 2½" x 8". Right sides together, sew trim to left front side of coat. Fold trim in half to the inside and slip-stitch in place. Cut trim even with coat bottom, if necessary. Slip-stitch bottom of front trim.

Step 12. Slip coat on snowman. Gather neck edge slightly, if necessary. Sew novelty buttons to front trim through all thicknesses. Position hat on head and glue to secure. Tie scarf around neck. Blush cheeks. ❄

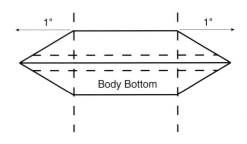

Fig. 1
Sew across seams as shown to create
flat snowman bottom.

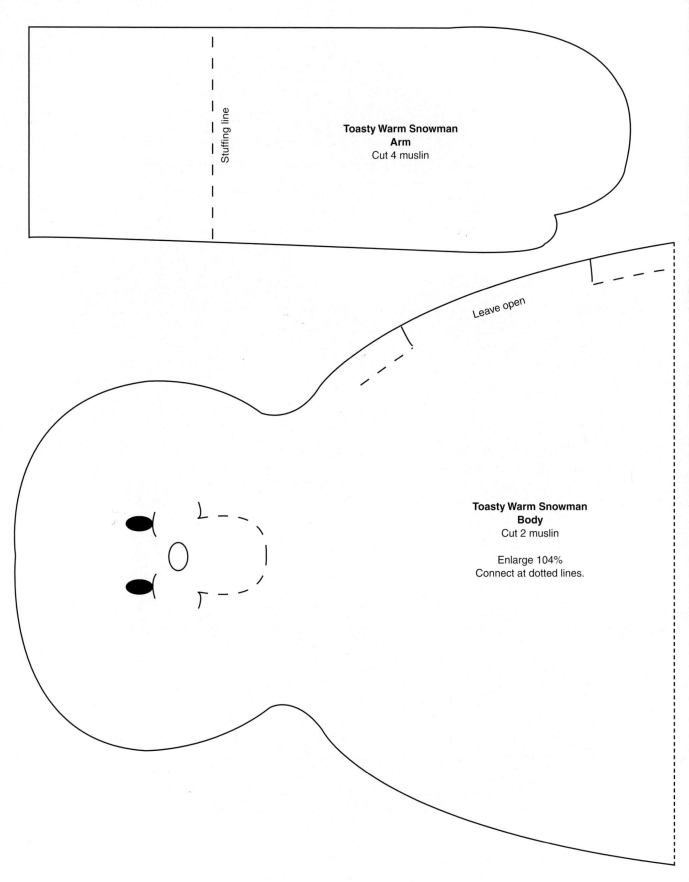

Toasty Warm Snowman
Arm
Cut 4 muslin

Stuffing line

Leave open

Toasty Warm Snowman
Body
Cut 2 muslin

Enlarge 104%
Connect at dotted lines.

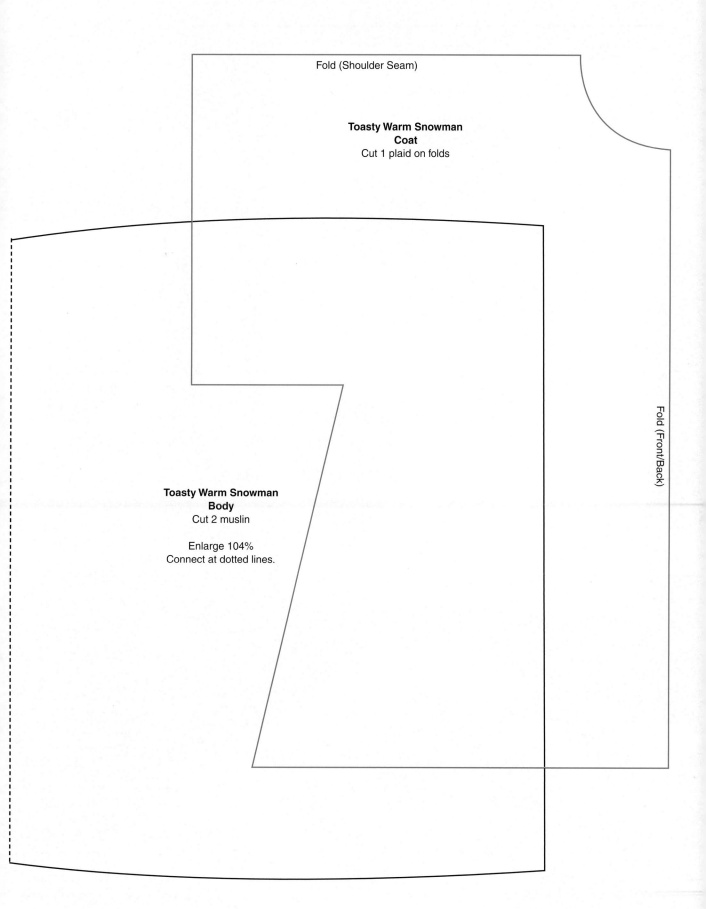

Fold (Shoulder Seam)

**Toasty Warm Snowman
Coat**
Cut 1 plaid on folds

Fold (Front/Back)

**Toasty Warm Snowman
Body**
Cut 2 muslin

Enlarge 104%
Connect at dotted lines.

STITCHED WITH LOVE

*O*h no! Christmas is in two days, and you don't have a gift for Aunt Lucy! And your officemates have decided at the last minute to have a gift exchange!

Not to worry, turn the pages of this chapter and find lots of projects that can be sewn lickety-split—just in time for those last-minute gift-giving occasions. There's something here for everyone, including you!

CRAZY QUILT TREASURE BOX

By Janice McKee

Every lady in your life—young or old—needs a safe place to keep treasures. Add special memories to your handmade gift by choosing fabric and trims with sentimental value.

Project Specifications

Skill Level: Beginner

Box Size: Approximately 7¼" x 7¼"

Materials

- 12" x 12" muslin foundation square
- Scraps of decorative fabrics: satins, brocades and velvets
- ⅓ yard dark green moiré fabric
- Scraps of laces and trims
- 6-strand black embroidery floss and other colors of your choice
- Fancy shank button
- Scraps of low-loft batting
- Heavy cardboard or mat board
- Glue stick
- Masking tape
- Freezer paper
- Basic sewing supplies and tools

Instructions

Step 1. Place a 2"–3" decorative fabric square, rectangle or pentagon on top of muslin foundation square. Position another irregular-shaped decorative fabric piece of approximately the same size face down on the first piece. Stitch along one edge with ¼" seam allowance. Flip open second piece of fabric and press flat.

Step 2. Stitch a piece of lace or trim over the seam line, or if you choose you may embroider by hand later.

Step 3. Continue to add fabrics and trims in this manner, adding them in a clockwise direction until muslin is covered.

Step 4. Hand-embroider any unadorned seams with feather stitch, buttonhole stitch or other decorative stitches of your choice. See Figs. 1–5.

Step 5. Cut rectangles and hexagons as directed on patterns.

Step 6. Use glue stick to glue batting to each cardboard piece.

Step 7. Place Crazy-Quilt-pieced fabric right side down on work surface. Center one cardboard hexagon on top, batting side down. Fold edges of fabric over cardboard and tape securely. Repeat with green moiré for box bottom.

Step 8. Cover rectangles each with a different decorative fabric as in Step 7.

Step 9. To line each box piece center freezer paper shiny side up on wrong side of lining fabric. Fold seam allowance over freezer paper and with tip of iron press seam allowance to freezer paper. (Be careful not to press exposed freezer paper or it will melt on your iron).

Step 10. Pin lining pieces to corresponding box pieces, covering raw edges of fabric and masking tape. Add pieces of batting between lining fabric and box pieces, if you wish. Slipstitch lining in place, removing freezer paper before stitching last side.

Step 11. With 2 strands of black embroidery floss, stitch box side pieces together with chevron stitch as shown in Fig. 5. Position assembled sides on top of

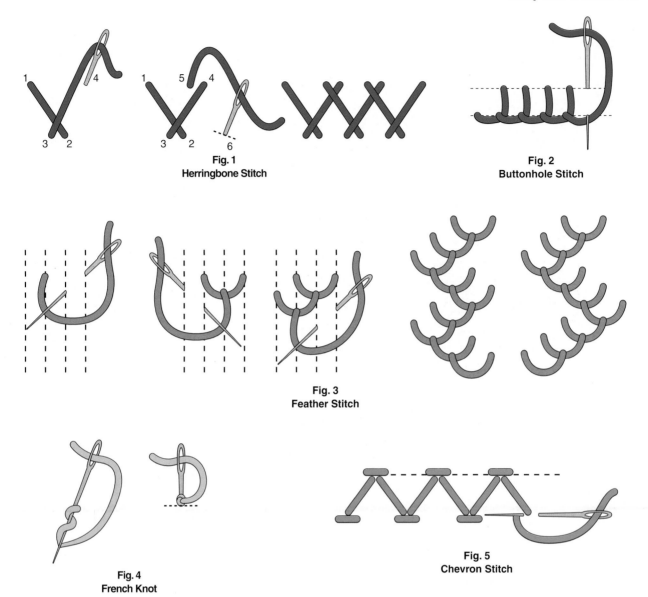

Fig. 1
Herringbone Stitch

Fig. 2
Buttonhole Stitch

Fig. 3
Feather Stitch

Fig. 4
French Knot

Fig. 5
Chevron Stitch

box bottom; pin in place and join with small whip stitch from the outside.

Step 12. For tassel, thread shank button with floss colors of your choice to coordinate with fabrics. Leave enough floss loop above shank to sew button to box top. Wind about 2½" of floss below the shank. Tie

around floss bundle below shank to secure; tie off.

Step 13. Attach button to box top so both button and tassel hang in front. Wind floss above shank to secure. Trim ends of tassel evenly.

Step 14. Stitch one side of box top to one side of box. ❀

Crazy Quilt Treasure Box
Top & Bottom
Cut 2 cardboard, 2 batting and 2
freezer paper same size as pattern

Cut 1 patchwork and 1 green moiré
1/2" larger all around

Cut 2 green moiré 1/4" larger all around

Crazy Quilt Treasure Box
Box Side
Cut 6 cardboard, 6 batting and 6
freezer paper same size as pattern

Cut 6 various decorative fabrics 3/8"
larger all around

Cut 6 green moiré 1/4" larger all around

HOLIDAY CHEER STATIONERY SET

By Barbara E. Swanson

Nice for almost anyone on your list—
college student, nursing-home resident,
favorite aunt—this stationery set will be
appreciated.

Project Specifications
Skill Level: Beginner
Stationery Holder Size: Approximately 8" x 11"

Materials
- ½ yard natural tone-on-tone fabric
- Scraps of yellow, green, blue and magenta fabric for appliqué
- ¼ yard fusible transfer web
- ½ yard fusible interfacing
- 9" x 12" tear-away stabilizer
- Machine-embroidery threads to match appliqués
- Gold metallic machine-embroidery thread
- 10" x 7" rectangles of yellow, green, blue and magenta card stock (or 5" x 7" cards)
- 10" x 7" sheets of ivory paper and matching envelopes
- Fine- and medium-tip gold metallic markers
- Fabric marker
- Glue stick
- Basic sewing supplies and tools

Instructions

STATIONERY HOLDER

Step 1. From natural tone-on-tone fabric cut two pieces 11½" x 16½" for stationery holder and lining. From fusible interfacing cut one piece the same size.

Step 2. Trace appliqué shapes on paper side of fusible transfer web as directed on patterns. Cut out leaving roughly ½" margin around shapes. Following manufacturer's directions fuse to selected fabrics. Cut out on traced lines. Trace design lines on ornaments.

Step 3. From natural tone-on-tone fabric cut stamp pocket 4⅛" x 4¾". From fusible interfacing cut one piece 2⅜" x 4⅛". Fuse to wrong side of one half of stamp pocket. Fold pocket in half with right sides facing. Stitch ¼" seam along sides and lower edge, leaving a 2" opening for turning. Trim and clip seam

allowance. Turn right side out and close opening with hand stitches; press.

Step 4. Cut flap as directed on pattern. Fuse interfacing to wrong side of one fabric piece. With right sides of fabric facing, pin pieces together. Stitch along top, angle and inside edge with ¼" seam allowance. Trim and clip seam allowance. Turn right side out and press.

Step 5. From natural tone-on-tone fabric cut one piece 2" x 2½" for pen loop. Cut fusible interfacing 1" x 2½" and fuse to wrong side of one half of pen loop.

Step 6. With right sides facing up, place stamp pocket on flap as indicated on pattern. Topstitch in place. Fold pen loop in half, right sides facing. Stitch ¼" seam along one side and lower edge, leaving one end open for turning. Trim and clip seam allowance. Turn right side out. Place finished end over cut end, forming loop. Pin to flap as indicated and topstitch in place.

Step 7. Right sides up, pin flap to lower right corner of stationery holder lining, aligning raw edges. Baste in place.

Step 8. Referring to photo for placement, fuse ornaments and hangers to right side of Stationery Holder. Pin stabilizer behind appliqué areas and machine-appliqué around edges with matching thread colors. Embroider designs with gold metallic thread. Mark a straight line from each ornament to top of holder. Stitch on line with gold metallic thread. Remove stabilizer.

Step 9. Fuse interfacing to wrong side of holder cover.

Step 10. Right sides together, pin cover and liner

together. Stitch ⅝" seam around perimeter leaving a 4" opening for turning. Trim and clip seam allowance. Turn right side out. Close opening with hand stitches; press.

PAPER

Step 1. Reduce and trace appliqué shapes on paper side of fusible transfer web as directed on patterns. Cut out leaving roughly ½" margin around shapes. Following manufacturer's directions fuse to selected fabrics. Cut out on traced lines. Trace design lines on ornaments.

Step 2. Cut one sheet of ivory paper into four pieces 3½" x 5". Referring to Fig. 1 for placement, fuse an ornament to each piece of paper with dry iron. Add stitching lines and designs with gold metallic markers.

Step 3. Fold colored card stock in half. Center designs on front of cards and glue in place. Cut four pieces 4½" x 6½" from paper sheets. Glue one to inside of each card for writing a greeting.

Step 4. Fuse an ornament to each of four ivory stationery sheets as shown in Fig. 2. Add details as in Step 2. ✾

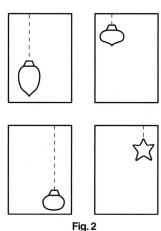

Fig. 2
Position ornaments and
add details as shown.

Holiday Cheer Stationery Set
Star
Cut 1 yellow for holder
Reduce 88% for paper
Cut 2 yellow

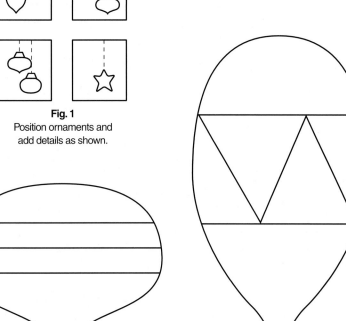

Fig. 1
Position ornaments and
add details as shown.

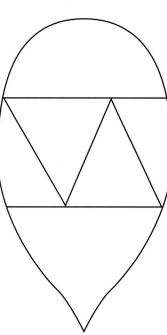

Holiday Cheer Stationery Set
Ornament
Cut 1 magenta for holder
Reduce 88% for paper
Cut 3 magenta

Holiday Cheer Stationery Set
Ornament
Cut 1 blue for holder
Reduce 88% for paper
Cut 2 blue

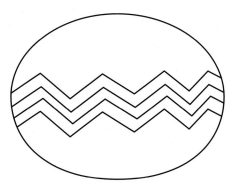

Holiday Cheer Stationery Set
Ornament
Cut 1 green for holder
Reduce 88% for paper
Cut 2 green

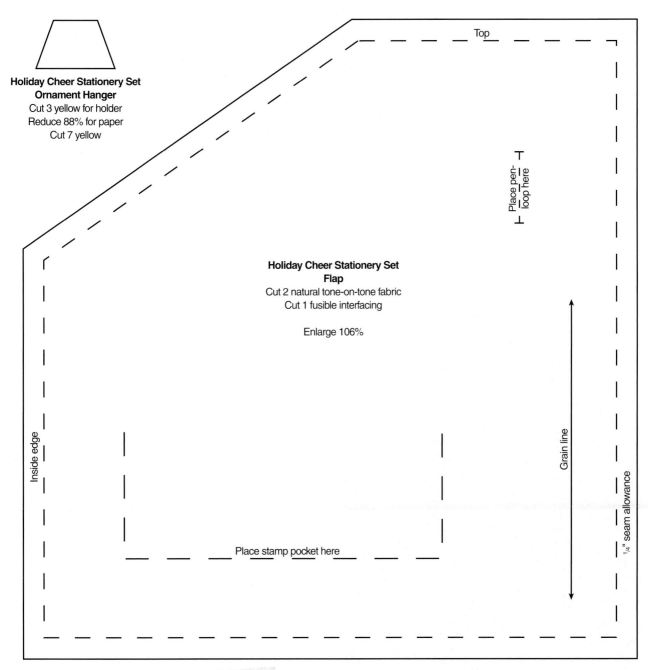

Holiday Cheer Stationery Set
Ornament Hanger
Cut 3 yellow for holder
Reduce 88% for paper
Cut 7 yellow

Top

Place pen-loop here

Holiday Cheer Stationery Set
Flap
Cut 2 natural tone-on-tone fabric
Cut 1 fusible interfacing

Enlarge 106%

Inside edge

Grain line

¹⁄₄" seam allowance

Place stamp pocket here

ANGEL TREE TOPPER

By June Fiechter

Imagine creating this beautiful angel to top your Christmas tree. It will certainly become a family heirloom and an important part of your traditional holiday memories.

Project Specifications
Skill Level: Beginner
Tree Topper Size: Approximately 17" x 10"

Materials
- 2" x 3" porcelain-look doll face
- Curly brown yarn doll hair
- 33" x 15½" textured ruby red felt
- 12½" x 19" textured hunter green felt
- 22" x 15" textured denim blue felt triangle
- 2 (11" x 16") pieces gold felt
- Unopened 2-piece package of 4" plastic foam snowballs
- 2½" plastic foam snowball
- 7" dowel rod ⅜" in diameter
- 2½"-diameter brass filigree for tiara
- 4" round white Battenburg lace doily
- 3 ceramic novelty buttons
- Hot-glue gun and glue
- All-purpose threads to match fabrics
- Liquid fabric stiffener
- 1" flat paintbrush
- Basic sewing supplies and tools

Instructions
Step 1. Press the 2½" plastic foam ball into the back of the doll face and hot-glue in place.

Step 2. Insert brass filigree into top of plastic foam ball behind face for tiara; secure with glue. Glue doll hair over plastic foam ball and around face.

Step 3. Cut wings as directed on pattern. Place pieces together and sew around perimeter leaving opening for turning. Turn right side out and close opening with hand stitches. Trace and topstitch lines shown on pattern. Paint wings with fabric stiffener and allow to dry.

Step 4. To make dress sew 15 evenly spaced pleats along one long edge of ruby red felt. Make pleats ¾" wide and 7" long. Cut away excess fabric and press. Right sides together, sew short ends together. Cut a small hole in center of doily and place over top of dress.

Step 5. For the body, push the dowel rod down through the unopened package of 4" snowballs with 3" protruding from top. Slide body under dress and through hole in doily. Attach dowel to head through 2½" ball. Hot-glue to hold.

Step 6. Stand body on a tall drinking glass to work with remaining felt.

Step 7. Wrap hunter green felt around shoulders for shawl. Stitch in place as if being held underneath by angel's hand.

Step 8. Sew or glue novelty buttons to front of shawl.

Step 9. Wrap blue triangle around head as a scarf. Hot-glue in place.

Step 10. Hot-glue wings to back of scarf. Drape red and blue felt attractively and paint with fabric stiffener. Allow to dry completely and place on top of Christmas tree. ✾

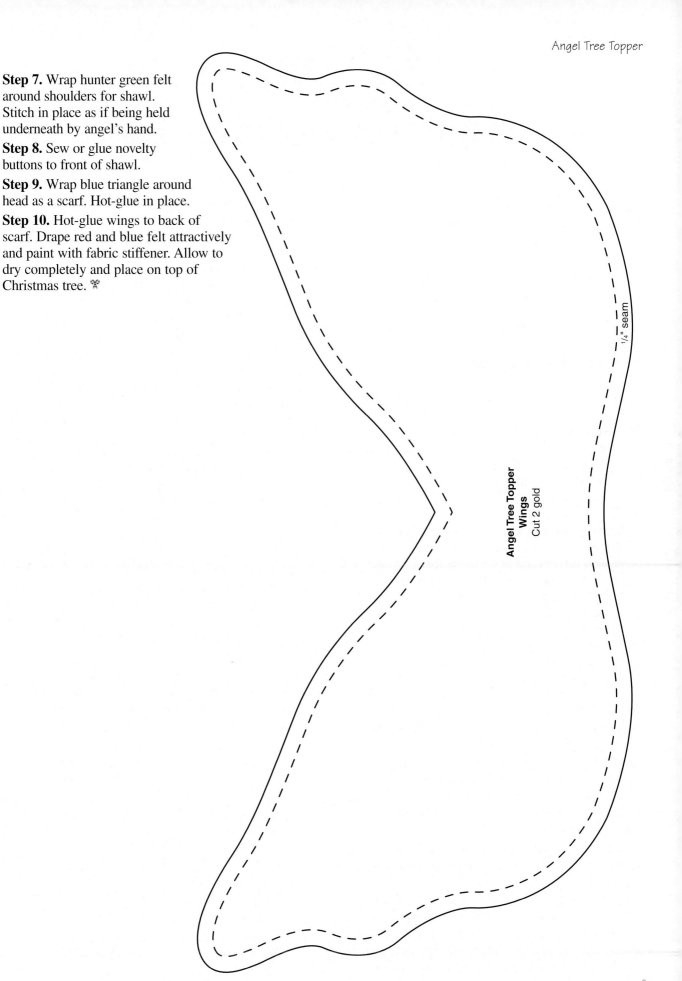

1/4" seam

Angel Tree Topper Wings
Cut 2 gold

CHRISTMAS TIC-TAC-TOE

By Barbara E. Swanson

There will certainly be giggles when Santas and reindeer show up on the game board. Pack this set away in its own bag with your Christmas decorations and it will be anticipated year after year.

Project Specifications

Skill Level: Beginner
Game Board Size: Approximately 14" x 14"

Materials

- ½ yard muslin
- ½ yard green broadcloth
- 12" x 18" red broadcloth
- Brown print scraps for reindeer
- Tan print scraps for antlers
- White-on-white scraps for Santa beard and hat
- Red print scraps for Santa's hat and reindeer nose
- 1 yard each red and green single-fold bias tape
- 1¼ yards extra-wide red double-fold bias tape
- 21" x 21" square low-loft batting
- 1 yard ¼"-wide red satin ribbon
- Black 6-strand embroidery floss
- Powdered cosmetic blush
- Cotton swab
- Basic sewing supplies and tools

Instructions

Step 1. Cut 10 squares each 3½" x 3½" from red broadcloth, green broadcloth and batting.

Step 2. Trace appliqué patterns on paper side of fusible transfer web as directed on patterns. Cut out leaving roughly ½" around traced lines. Following manufacturer's instructions, fuse to selected fabrics. Cut out on traced lines.

Step 3. Referring to photo for placement, arrange five reindeer on red squares and five Santas on green squares. Fuse in place.

Step 4. With three strands of black embroidery floss, stitch reindeer mouth with a single straight stitch. Using six strands of floss make French knots for eyes. Pin a square of batting to the wrong side of appliquéd square and baste in place. Right sides facing, pin a plain red square to an appliquéd square. Stitch a ¼" seam around the square, leaving a 1¾" opening for turning. Trim seam, clip corners and turn right side out. Close opening with hand stitches. Repeat for a total of five reindeer squares.

Step 5. Create Santa squares in same manner as Step 4. Use three strands of floss for French knot eyes. Brush nose with cotton swab and cosmetic blush.

Step 6. Cut one rectangle 20½" x 16½" from green broadcloth. Right sides together, fold in half bringing short ends together. Stitch ¼" seam along one short side (bottom). Stitch 12¼" up the long side. Leave a ¾" opening, then stitch the remaining 3½" to the top edge. Trim and clip seam. Press a ¼" hem at top edge. Press a 2" header toward the inside and pin in place. Stitch along the edge of the casing. Stitch again ¾" away to form the casing for the ribbon. Referring to photo, fuse remaining reindeer and Santa to front of bag and finish details as in Steps 4 and 5. Weave red ribbon through casing.

Step 7. Cut two 14" x 14" squares from muslin and one from batting. Measure and mark a line 4¾" from left edge of one muslin square. Cut red and green single-fold bias tape in half. Center one green piece over line and topstitch in place. Mark another line 4¾" from right edge and stitch remaining green tape over that line.

Step 8. Repeat with red tape, marking lines 4¾" from top and bottom edges.

Step 9. Wrong sides facing, sandwich batting between two muslin squares. Baste edges together. Bind edges with extra-wide red double-fold bias tape, mitering corners. ❄

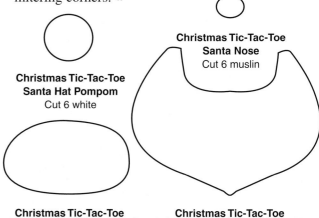

**Christmas Tic-Tac-Toe
Santa Hat Pompom**
Cut 6 white

**Christmas Tic-Tac-Toe
Santa Nose**
Cut 6 muslin

**Christmas Tic-Tac-Toe
Santa Face**
Cut 6 muslin

**Christmas Tic-Tac-Toe
Santa Beard**
Cut 6 white

**Christmas Tic-Tac-Toe
Reindeer Nose**
Cut 6 red

**Christmas Tic-Tac-Toe
Reindeer Antlers**
Cut 12 tan

**Christmas Tic-Tac-Toe
Santa Hat**
Cut 6 red

**Christmas Tic-Tac-Toe
Santa Hat Cuff**
Cut 6 white

**Christmas Tic-Tac-Toe
Reindeer Face**
Cut 6 brown

PIN PILLOWS

By Connie Matricardi

Nearly every room in the house needs a repository for pins and it might as well be beautiful and large enough to find when needed. Any or all of these pretty pillows are big enough for the job.

Project Specifications

Skill Level: Beginner

Size: rectangle, 4" x 7½"; square, 5" x 5"; heart, 6" x 6"; oval, 5" x 8"

Materials

- ¼ yard cotton or cotton blend for each pillow in color of your choice
- 23" length of coordinating cording (also called welting or piping) for each pillow
- Additional 18" length of cording for hanging pillows
- 4 (1") tassels for rectangle pillow
- Small ribbon rose for heart pillow
- All-purpose threads to match fabrics
- Polyester fiberfill
- Basic sewing supplies and tools

Instructions

Step 1. Cut pillow shapes as directed on patterns.

Step 2. Beginning at rectangle or square side center, or lower center of heart or oval, pin cording to pillow front, right sides facing. Be certain that cording edge

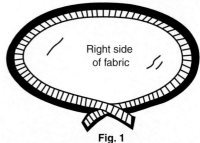

Fig. 1

Pin cording to pillow top as shown with ends overlapping.

faces center of pillow. Overlap ends where cording meets as shown in Fig. 1.

Step 3. *On rectangle pillow only* tack a tassel at each corner with tassels facing the center of the cushion as shown in Fig. 2.

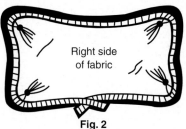

Right side of fabric

Fig. 2
Tack tassels to corners of rectangle pillow as shown.

Step 4. *On hanging pillows only* position and pin 18" cording ends in place. Be certain that entire length of cording is inside the pillow when sewing.

Step 5. With a zipper foot on the sewing machine, baste the cording in place. Stitch as close to the cording as possible.

Step 6. Generously pin pillow front to pillow back, right sides together. Pin through cording. Use zipper foot to stitch pillow front to pillow back, leaving a 3½" opening for turning. Ease fabric where needed. Remove pins as you sew.

Step 7. Turn pillow right side out. Stuff firmly and evenly with polyester fiberfill. Close openings with hand stitches. Tack ribbon rose to cleft of heart pillow. ❧

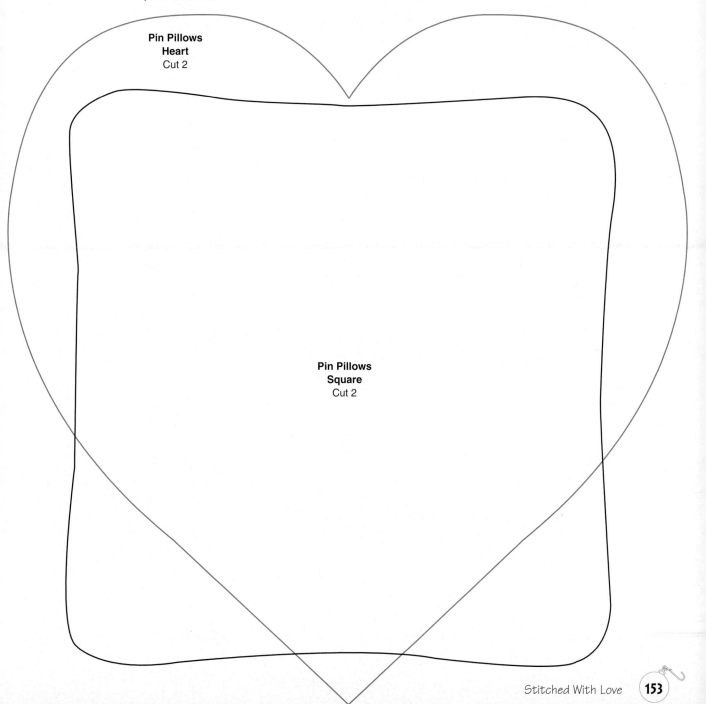

**Pin Pillows
Heart
Cut 2**

**Pin Pillows
Square
Cut 2**

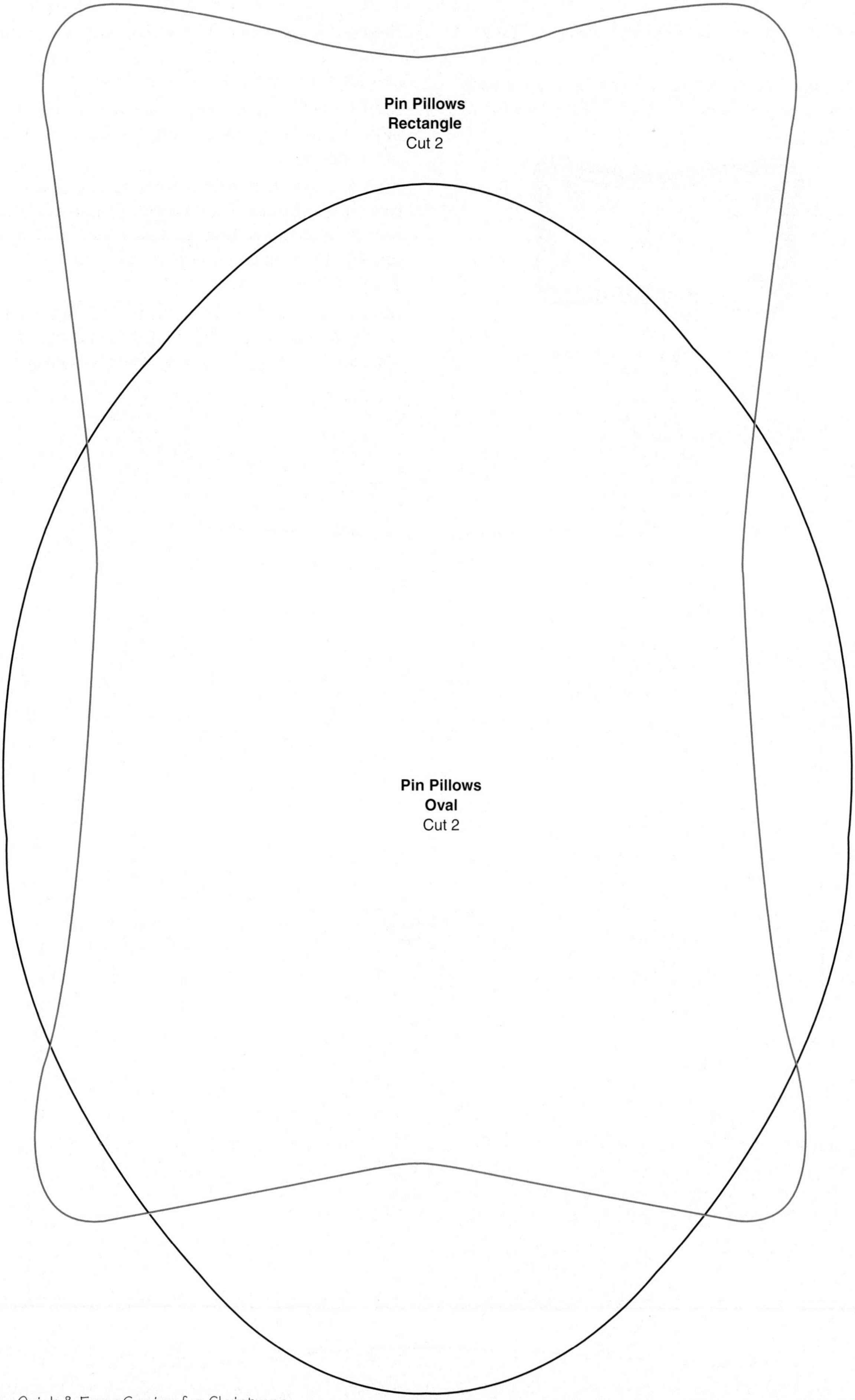

**Pin Pillows
Rectangle
Cut 2**

**Pin Pillows
Oval
Cut 2**

DADDY'S OLD TIES CLUTCH PURSE

By Marian Shenk

The silk fabrics in neckties are too beautiful to discard. Coordinate your lucky finds with pretty trims and create a lovely original purse.

Project Specifications
Skill Level: Beginner
Purse Size: Approximately 10" x 6½" x 1½"

Materials
• 4 recycled silk neckties
• ½ yard muslin foundation fabric
• ½ yard coordinating cotton print lining fabric
• 1 (⅞") decorative button
• 2 yards coordinating cord piping
• ⅝ yard 1½"-wide satin ribbon
• 1 hook-and-loop circle for fastener
• All-purpose threads to match fabrics
• Basic sewing supplies and tools

Instructions
Step 1. Enlarge pattern 222 percent; cut one lining and one muslin foundation from enlarged pattern.

Step 2. Remove stitches from neckties and press open. Cut into 2"-wide strips.

Step 3. Starting at the top center point of bag sew a strip right side up on each side of center as shown in Fig. 1.

Step 4. Place next strips on top of first strips right sides together and sew. Flip open and press. Continue to sew and flip strips down each side of center until foundation is covered.

Step 5. Place satin ribbon over raw edges at center. Place piping edge under ribbon on each side. Machine-overcast each side of ribbon.

Step 6. Right sides together, place lining piece on top and sew across straight end. Pin piping around angled flap of purse. With lining over piping, sew layers together around flap, leaving sides open.

Step 7. Turn right side out. Fold bottom of purse, right sides together, up to piping. Sew side seams without catching the front of the lining from the fold up. Hand-stitch front lining over raw edges.

Step 8. Match side seams and center bottom. Sew

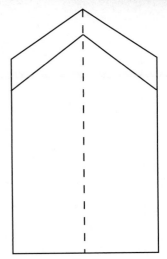

Fig. 1
Sew strips to each side
of center as shown.

Fig. 2
Stitch across ends as
shown to box bottom.

across points as shown in Fig. 2. Turn right side out.

Step 9. Sew hook-and-loop fastener pieces in place. Sew decorative button to outside of purse over fastener. ✤

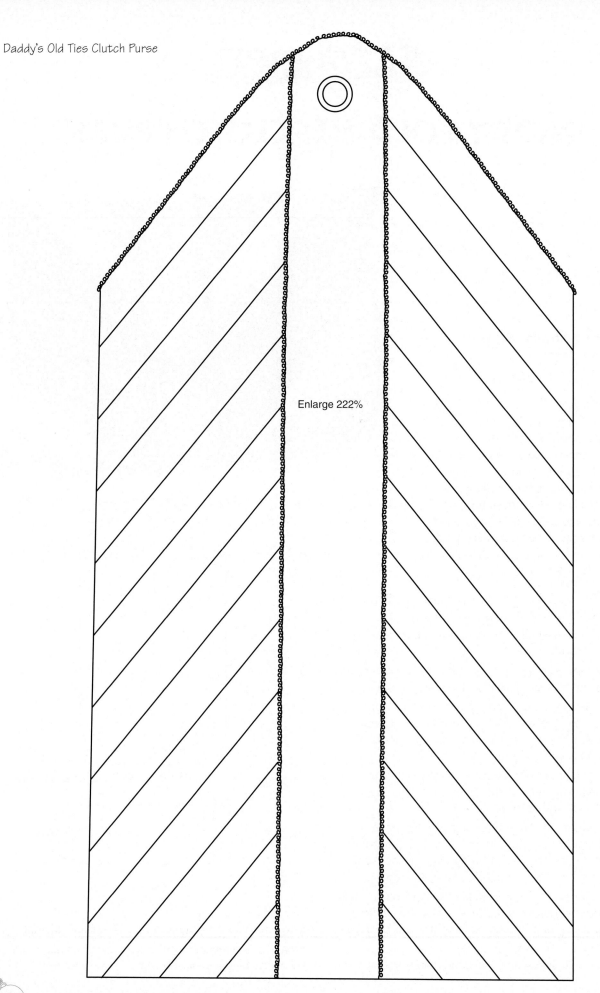

Enlarge 222%

HOLIDAY SPARKLE JEWELRY SET

By Donna Friebertshauser

Surprise your friends when you wear designer jewelry—created by you! Match a favorite outfit or create an outfit to complement the jewelry.

Project Specifications
Skill Level: Beginner
Size: Any Size

Materials
• 3" x 36" strip of soft solid or mini-print
Note: An increase in the number and size of beads will require more fabric.
• 1 skein metallic gold embroidery floss
• 11 or more purchased or recycled beads
• All-purpose thread to match fabric
• Button and carpet thread, beading thread, dental floss or fine cord for stringing beads
• Embroidery #7 or similar fine needle
• Milliner's #3, darner or other long, sharp needle
• ½ yard rattail or decorative cord to match fabric
• H or K crochet hook
• Polyester fiberfill
• Plastic scraps from milk carton or product lid
• Pair of earring backs or wires
• Clear-drying craft glue
• Toothpick
• Commercial fabric stiffener
• Basic sewing supplies and tools

Instructions

BEADS

Step 1. Each bead requires a 2" x 2" square of fabric. Determine number of beads desired and draw that number of 2" squares on fabric. Do not cut apart. It is easier to work with a larger piece of fabric.

Step 2. Each bead should be original, so do not trace design on fabric square. Referring to Figs. 1 and 2, stitch various-size lazy-daisy stitches radiating from center of one square. Sew with a 12"–15" single strand of gold metallic thread.

Step 3. Inside each lazy daisy work a single straight stitch to fill the space. Between lazy daisy stitches work more straight stitches of different lengths. Fig. 2

Fig. 1
Lazy-Daisy Stitch

Fig. 2
Sample stitch placement.

shows a sample placement of stitches, but choose your own preferred placement.

Step 4. Referring to Fig. 3, fill the center of the design with several French knots.

Step 5. Repeat for desired number of beads. Cut 2" squares apart.

Step 6. On opposite sides of each square, fold ⅛" seam allowance to back of fabric and finger press.

Step 7. Right sides together, fold other two sides of each square together. Stitch by hand or machine with ⅛" seam allowance to form tubes. Use crochet hook to turn tubes right side out.

Step 8. With matching all-purpose thread and small running stitches, sew around one end of each bead. Pull up thread to gather and close the end of bead. Securely fasten thread and cut.

Step 9. Stuff each bead with polyester fiberfill, using end of crochet hook to firmly fill.

Step 10. When bead is filled close remaining end as in Step 8.

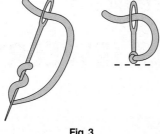

**Fig. 3
French Knot**

MEDALLION

Step 1. Trace and cut medallion as directed on pattern. On fabric piece including seam allowance repeat Steps 2–4 above, slightly elongating the design to fit oval. Run a small basting stitch around the shape. Do not fasten thread.

Step 2. Place a small amount of polyester fiberfill on the plastic oval. Place embroidered oval on top and pull up basting threads around plastic. Weave basting thread back and forth across back as shown in Fig. 4 until fabric is taut.

Step 3. Stiffen smaller fabric oval with fabric stiffener.

Fig. 4
Weave basting thread
as shown to secure.

Trim shape slightly smaller than embroidered oval if necessary. Glue to back of medallion.

EARRINGS

Step 1. Determine preferred earring size and cut two circles of fabric and one circle of plastic for each earring. Add ⅛" seam allowance to the circle to be embroidered.

Step 2. Embroider and finish as for Medallion. Glue earring backs to each earring.

NECKLACE

Step 1. With milliner's needle and chosen stringing thread, place a commercial bead on needle. Leave a length of stringing thread for attaching cord later. Go through center of one embroidered bead. Continue to alternate to center of medallion. Add two commercial beads, stitch into medallion to secure. Go back through last commercial bead, through another commercial bead and repeat stringing as for first side of necklace. Keep needle threaded at end of stringing.

Step 2. Cut two 7" lengths of rattail or cord (longer if necessary to fit). Tie a knot 1" from each end of each piece. Fold one 1" end back against cord. With stringing material, sew through knot and securely fasten to stringing thread. Repeat at other end. Stabilize all four cut ends of rattail or cord with clear glue. ❦

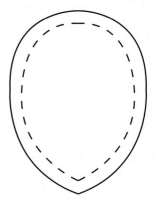

**Holiday Sparkle Jewelry Set
Medallion**
Cut 1 fabric with seam allowance
Cut 1 plastic and 1 fabric without
seam allowance

TEACHER'S HELPER DOLL

By Chris Malone

Appropriate yet special gifts for teachers are often difficult to find. This easy-to-make little miss is a memorable treasure.

Project Specifications

Skill Level: Beginner

Doll Size: Approximately 12" tall

Materials

- ½ yard unbleached muslin
- ¼ yard red-and-black check for body/blouse
- 6½" x 20½" school print for skirt
- Polyester fiberfill
- 2 (3mm) black beads
- Black 6-strand embroidery floss
- 3 yards craft hair
- 5" (½"-wide) white lace
- 2 (½") black buttons
- 1 (¾") red heart shank button (shank removed)
- ½ yard ⅜"-wide novelty ribbon to coordinate with skirt
- 8" (⅛"-wide) black satin ribbon
- 4" length of 20-gauge shiny black wire
- 2" wood-framed slate
- ½" wooden or plastic apple
- Bamboo skewer
- Black, white, green and pink acrylic paints
- Small round and liner paintbrushes
- Powdered cosmetic blush
- Cotton swab
- Clear permanent craft glue
- All-purpose threads to match fabrics
- Basic sewing supplies and tools

Instructions

DOLL

Step 1. From muslin cut one strip 2½" x 7½" for head and one strip 1½" x 5" for hands. From checked fabric cut one strip 5½" x 7½" for body and one strip 4½" x 5" for arms.

Step 2. Sew head and body strips together along one 7½" edge; press seam allowance toward body. Right sides together, fold strip in half matching seamlines. Trace head/body pattern on doubled fabric, neckline at

seam. Pin to secure and sew around perimeter, leaving open at bottom where indicated on pattern. Trim seams to ⅛", clip curves and turn right side out. Stuff firmly with polyester fiberfill and set aside.

Step 3. Sew arm and hand pieces together along one 5" edge; press seam allowance toward arm fabric. Right sides together, fold strip in half matching seam lines. Trace arm/hand pattern twice on doubled fabric, wrist at seamline. Stitch on traced lines leaving open at top. Trim seams to ⅛", clip curves and turn right side out. Stuff firmly with polyester fiberfill and close opening with hand stitches.

Step 4. Sew black button to top of arm, then sew arm

and button to shoulder in position indicated on body pattern. Repeat for other arm.

Step 5. Trace leg pattern twice on doubled muslin. Stitch on traced lines, leaving open at top. Stuff firmly with polyester fiberfill. Use black acrylic paint and round brush to paint shoes on feet. Let dry.

Step 6. Insert tops of legs in body opening, toes pointing out. Close opening with hand stitches, catching legs in seam.

Step 7. Use one strand of black embroidery floss to sew beads in place for eyes and to make straight stitches for eyebrows and nose line. Make beginning and ending knots at top of head where they will be covered by hair. Blush cheeks with cotton swab.

Step 8. Cut hair in 10" pieces. Using thread that matches hair, take one stitch in top of head. Wrap one length of hair around two fingers three times. Hold looped hair to top of head and take a stitch over center of bundle; pull thread snug. Insert needle back into head and come out about ⅜" to one side; sew on another hair bundle. Repeat down both sides of head and on back till head is fully covered. Tack or trim any loose ends.

Step 9. Right sides together, sew short ends of skirt fabric together and press seam open. Press and sew a double ¼" hem along one long edge. Press a 1" hem at top edge. Machine- or hand-sew gathering stitches ¾" from fold. Slip skirt on body. Pull gathers so skirt fits snugly; knot and clip thread. Wrap novelty ribbon around waist, covering stitches, and tie in a bow at center front. Tie a knot in each end and trim at a slant.

Step 10. Glue white lace around neck, overlapping ends slightly in back. Glue heart to neck front.

Step 11. Cut black satin ribbon in half. Tie each half in a small bow; trim ends at a slant. Glue each bow to top of a shoe.

ACCESSORIES

Step 1. Thin white paint slightly with water and use liner brush to write "ABC" and "123" on slate. Dip brush handle or toothpick into regular-consistency white paint and touch to ends of letters for dots as shown in Fig. 1. Let dry. Glue apple to corner of slate and glue slate to inside of one arm.

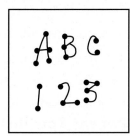

Fig. 1
Paint slate as shown.

Step 2. Cut a 2" piece from pointed end of bamboo skewer for pencil. Paint ⅛" pink around end for eraser. Paint body of pencil green, leaving ⅜" at pointed tip natural. Paint point black for lead and paint a black stripe between eraser and pencil. Let dry. Poke pencil into hair and secure with dot of glue.

Step 3. For glasses wrap wire around pencil once, 1" from end of wire. Leave a straight section ⅜" long and wrap around pencil again. Push straight ends back from circles and poke ends into hair. If desired, put a dot of glue on ends before inserting to hold in place.

Note: *Other miniature accessories can be substituted to personalize the doll.* ❀

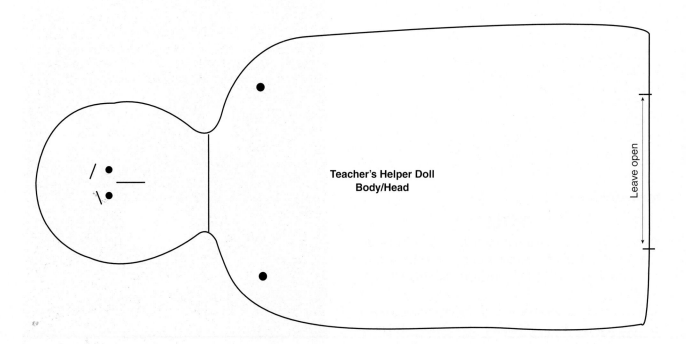

**Teacher's Helper Doll
Body/Head**

Leave open

Patterns continued on page 165

KITTY & DOGGIE BIBS

By Kathy Brown

With such wonderful, soft, washable fleece, why not give bibs some extra fun and dimension?

Project Specifications
Skill Level: Beginner
Bib Size: Approximately 10" x 13½"

Materials
- ½ yard gray plush felt for kitty
- ½ yard white fake fur for doggie
- Scraps of black-and-white spotted fleece for doggie ears
- Pink and white fabric scraps
- Fusible transfer web scraps
- 16" x 16" batting square for each
- All-purpose threads to match fabrics
- Snap or hook-and-loop circle for closure of each bib
- Air-soluble marker
- Black, pink and white acrylic paint
- Small craft paintbrush
- Basic sewing supplies and tools

Instructions

KITTY

Step 1. Cut bib fabric, batting and ears as directed on patterns.

Step 2. Trace eye shapes and nose on paper side of fusible transfer web. Cut out leaving roughly ¼" margin around each. Following manufacturer's directions, fuse eyes to white scraps and nose to pink scrap. Cut out on traced lines. Referring to photo for placement, fuse to bib front.

Step 3. Pin bib front to batting. With coordinating threads, machine-appliqué around each piece with nar-row satin stitch. With pink thread, satin-stitch a vertical straight line below nose for mouth line.

Step 4. Place two ear pieces right sides together. Stitch around edges leaving open on straight edge. Turn right side out. Repeat for second ear. Referring to pattern, pin to bib where indicated.

Step 5. Right sides together, pin bib front and back together. Stitch around perimeter leaving an opening for turning. Turn right side out and press. Close opening with hand stitches.

Step 6. Add closure of choice to top edges.

Step 7. Referring to photo and pattern, paint center of eye black; paint nose pink. When dry, add small white highlights.

DOGGIE

Step 1. Cut bib fabric, batting and ears as directed on pattern.

Step 2. Trace eye shapes, nose and tongue on paper side of fusible transfer web. Cut out leaving roughly ¼" margin around each. Following manufacturer's directions, fuse eyes and nose to black areas on spotted fleece. Fuse nose and tongue to pink scraps. Cut out on traced lines. Referring to photo for placement, fuse to bib front.

Step 3. With air-soluble marker trace doggie muzzle and mouth on face. Pin bib front to batting. With coordinating threads, machine-appliqué around each piece with narrow satin stitch. With black thread, satin-stitch a muzzle and mouth.

Step 4. Place right sides of two ear pieces together. Stitch around perimeter leaving flat end open. Turn right side out. Repeat for second ear. Stitch each ear in place in position indicated on pattern.

Step 5. Repeat Kitty Steps 5 and 6. With white paint highlight each eye as shown on pattern; paint tongue pink. ❦

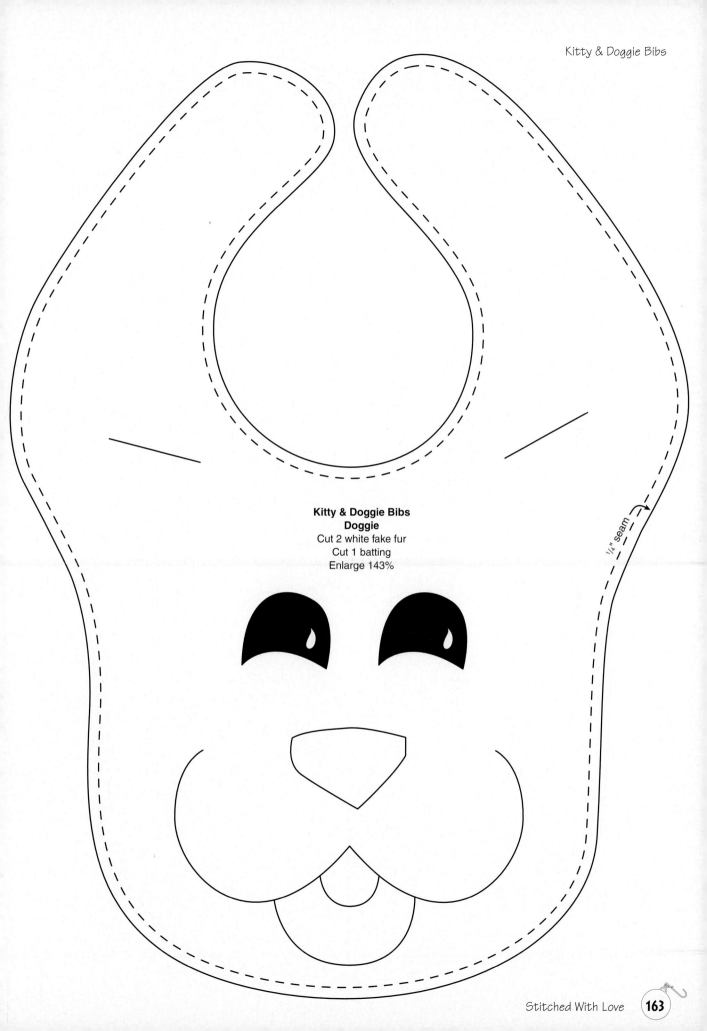

Kitty & Doggie Bibs
Doggie
Cut 2 white fake fur
Cut 1 batting
Enlarge 143%

¼" seam

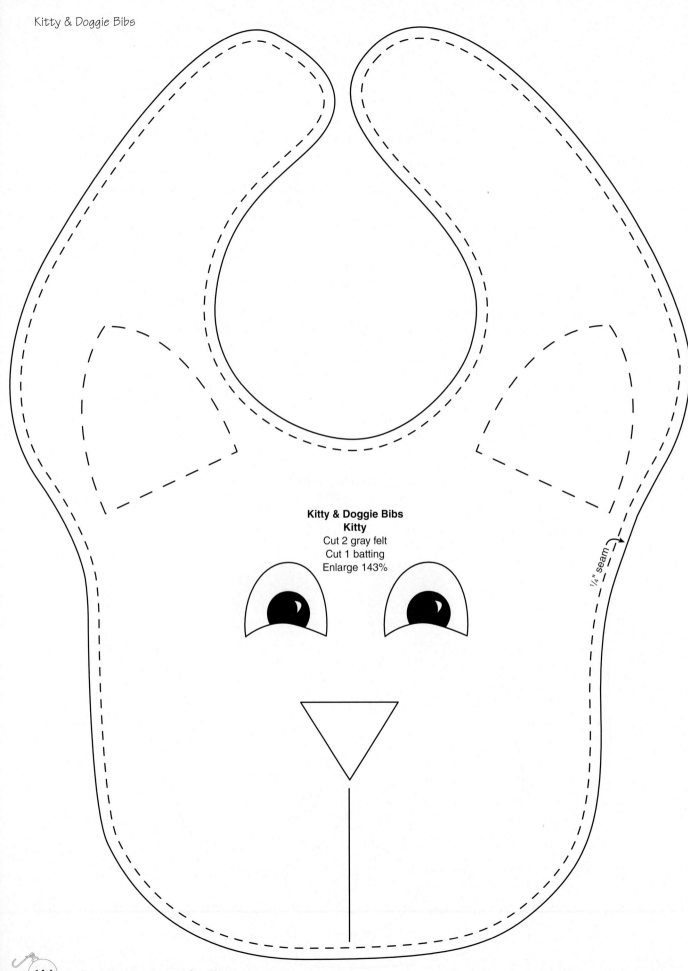

Kitty & Doggie Bibs
Kitty
Cut 2 gray felt
Cut 1 batting
Enlarge 143%

¼" seam

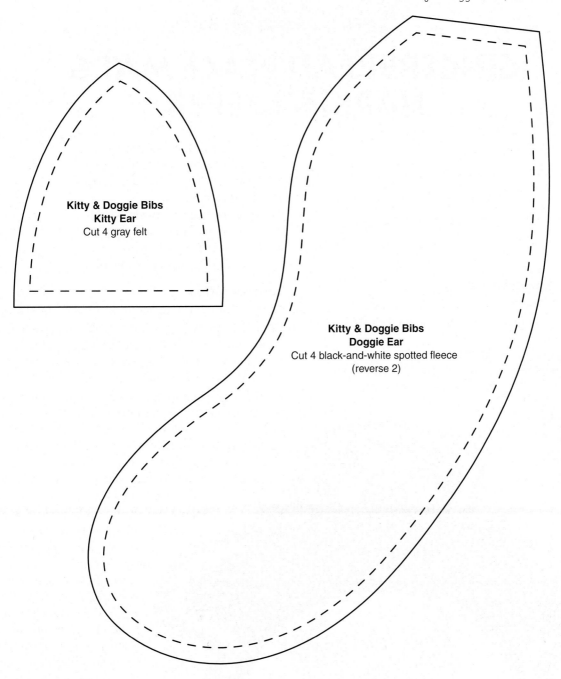

**Kitty & Doggie Bibs
Kitty Ear**
Cut 4 gray felt

**Kitty & Doggie Bibs
Doggie Ear**
Cut 4 black-and-white spotted fleece
(reverse 2)

Teacher's Helper Doll

Continued from page 160

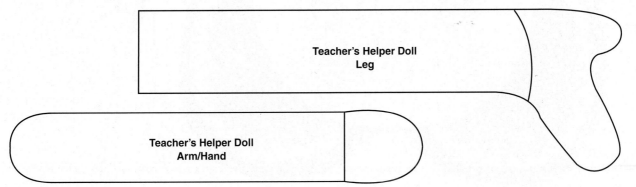

**Teacher's Helper Doll
Leg**

**Teacher's Helper Doll
Arm/Hand**

GINGERBREAD PLACE MAT & NAPKIN KEEPER

By Janice Loewenthal

'Tis the season to delight young and old, and you certainly will when meals are served on this spunky little gingerbread mat. Add your own napkin and you have an ensemble.

Project Specifications
Skill Level: Beginner

Place Mat Size: Approximately 16" x 13"

Materials
Note: Materials listed are for three place mats.

- 1 yard gingerbread-brown fabric
- Scraps of white and pink fabric
- 2 packages white medium rickrack
- ½ yard batting
- Scraps of fusible transfer web
- All-purpose threads to match fabrics
- 3 purchased plaid napkins
- Basic sewing supplies and tools

Instructions
Step 1. Cut fabric and batting as directed on pattern.

Step 2. Trace eyes, nose and cheeks on paper side of fusible transfer web. Cut out leaving roughly ½" margin around pieces. Following manufacturer's directions, fuse to selected fabrics.

Step 3. Referring to photo for placement, arrange pieces on one place mat fabric piece. Eyes and nose are the same shape. Eyes are placed vertically. Nose is placed horizontally. Trace a smile line from cheek to cheek. With a narrow satin stitch, sew on line with white thread. Machine-appliqué around eyes, nose and cheeks with matching threads.

Step 4. Place place mat fabric pieces right sides together. Place batting on wrong side of fabric. Stitch around perimeter with ¼" seam allowance. Leave an opening for turning at the top of the head. Clip curves and turn right side out; press. Close opening with hand stitches.

Step 5. Stitch rickrack around outer edge of place mat.

Step 6. For each place mat cut a strip of fabric 3" x 4½". Fold lengthwise, right sides together, and stitch long edge. Turn right side out and position seam down

center of one side. Turn each end under ¼" and press.

Step 7. Center one narrow end of strip ¼" below mouth. Stitch to mat. Position the other end 1½" below and stitch to mat, forming a loop.

Step 8. Fold napkin in half. Fold accordion style and insert in loop to form a bow tie. ✣

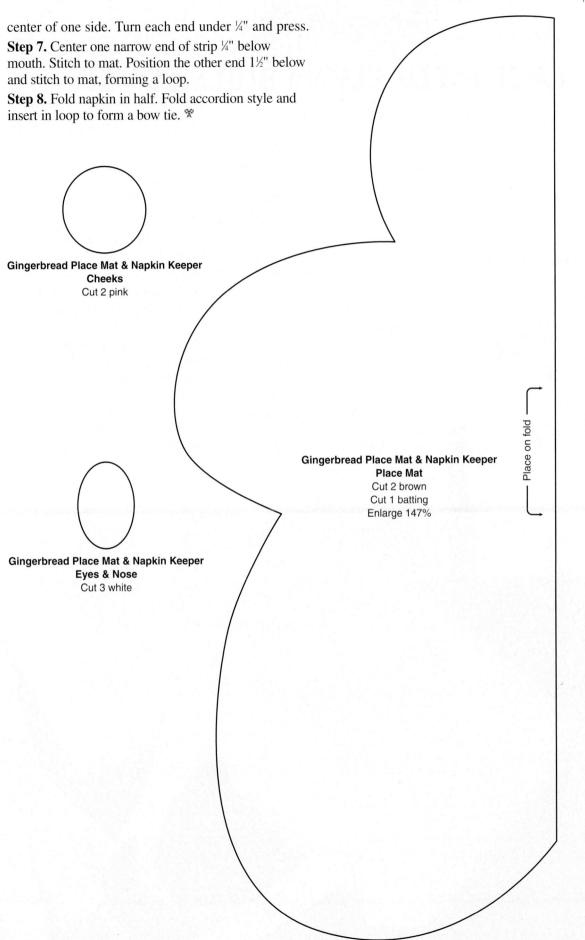

**Gingerbread Place Mat & Napkin Keeper
Cheeks**
Cut 2 pink

**Gingerbread Place Mat & Napkin Keeper
Eyes & Nose**
Cut 3 white

**Gingerbread Place Mat & Napkin Keeper
Place Mat**
Cut 2 brown
Cut 1 batting
Enlarge 147%

← Place on fold →

LACE MEDALLION BIBLE COVER

By Marian Shenk

A very thoughtful gift for someone dear to you or perhaps a special gift to yourself to protect your family Bible.

Project Specifications
Skill Level: Beginner
Bible Cover Size: Any size

Materials
- ½ yard fabric for cover
- ½ yard fabric for lining
- 1 lace medallion
- 1 purchased ribbon flower
- 2 yards ¾"-wide gathered lace
- ½ yard light batting
- All-purpose thread to match fabric
- Basic sewing supplies and tools

Instructions

Step 1. Place open Bible on cover fabric and cut one piece 1" larger all around. Cut one lining and one batting piece the same size.

Step 2. To make a pocket on the Bible cover back, cut one piece of cover fabric, lining and batting the width of the back cover and half its height.

Step 3. Right sides together, place pocket lining on pocket cover fabric and batting. Sew across top and down right side with ¼" seam. Turn right side out and press.

Step 4. Place pocket on lower left side of main cover fabric, aligning raw edges; pin. Place on cover batting piece. Pin gathered edge of lace around outer edges and sew around perimeter.

Continued on page 172

MY BUDDY 'N' ME JUMPERS

By Beth Wheeler

Mother-and-daughter outfits are so much fun, but take it one "generation" further and delight a little girl with matching wearables for herself and her doll. Guaranteed to be a smashing-success gift.

Project Specifications

Skill Level: Beginner

Child's Dress Size: Any size

Doll Dress Size: To fit 18" doll

Project Notes: Choose any child's unfitted jumper pattern with a button-front opening and a full skirt. We used Butterick 5167, size 7.

The doll dress fits most 18" dolls. Be aware that the torso of 18" dolls may vary. Some are designed with children's proportions while others have adult proportions. Those dolls with thicker or thinner torsos may require adjustments in the bodice pattern.

Child's dress is constructed with ⅝" seam allowance; doll's dress is constructed with ⅜" seam allowance.

Materials

- Commercial jumper pattern
- 2 red prints, yardage according to pattern (approximately ¼ of the fabric is for trim fabric and ¾ for primary fabric)
- Variety of yellow scraps
- ¼ yard fusible transfer web
- 3 (¾") black buttons
- Red and black all-purpose thread
- Black rayon machine-embroidery thread
- 1 package black jumbo piping
- 3 tiny black buttons for doll dress
- 3 small snaps
- 1 package small black piping
- Single-fold narrow black bias tape
- Basic sewing supplies and tools

Instructions

CHILD'S DRESS

Step 1. From trim fabric cut one bodice back and one front. Across the width of the fabric cut two trim strips 4½" and two ties (if there are any).

Step 2. From the primary fabric cut the other bodice front and skirt.

Step 3. Construct jumper bodice following pattern instructions. Insert black jumbo piping at neck and down center front, around armholes and around lower edge of bodice where it will join the skirt.

Step 4. On paper side of fusible transfer web, trace stars as directed on pattern. Cut out leaving roughly ½" margin around pieces. Fuse to selected fabrics following manufacturer's directions. Cut out on traced lines.

Step 5. Referring to photo, position two stars on primary-fabric side of bodice front and fuse.

Step 6. Join the two 4½" strips cut in Step 1 on one short edge; press seam open. Measure lower edge of skirt front and back (including seam allowance). Cut strip to that measured length.

Step 7. Referring to photo to placement, fuse remaining stars to strip.

Step 8. Sew skirt pieces together, leaving one side seam open. Press seams open.

Step 9. Position border strip with stars on skirt, matching seam allowance of border with seam allowance of skirt. Wrong side of border strip should face right side of skirt and raw edge of border should be 2¼" above hemline (not raw edge) of skirt. Stitch each edge to skirt with straight stitch to hold in place.

Step 10. With black rayon machine-embroidery thread in the needle and black all-purpose thread in the bobbin, satin-stitch around each star.

Step 11. Position single-fold narrow black tape over raw edges of border strip. Stitch close to each fold.

Step 12. Stitch remaining side seam, and complete construction of jumper according to manufacturer's directions. Hem skirt.

DOLL DRESS

Step 1. Cut bodice as directed on pattern. Cut one skirt piece 8" x 28" from primary fabric. Cut one border piece 2" x 28" from trim fabric.

Step 2. Cut two strips 1½" x 15" for ties. Fold in half lengthwise and stitch along long edge and across one end. Turn and press.

Step 3. Stitch two different fronts and one back together for bodice shell, inserting ties at bodice side

seams. Stitch remaining two fronts and back together for lining. Stitch shell and lining together, inserting small black piping around neckline, center front and armholes. Turn right side out and press.

Step 4. Sew small black piping around lower edge of bodice where it will join the skirt.

Step 5. Stitch small snaps in button positions. Stitch buttons on right side of bodice as worn.

Step 6. Cut stars as directed on pattern and fuse to fabrics as in Step 4, Child's Dress. Fuse one star to bodice front. Fuse remaining stars to border strip cut in Step 1. Position border strip 1½" from one long raw edge of skirt. Stitch to hold in place. Position single-fold narrow black bias tape over raw edges of border strip; stitch close to each fold.

Step 7. With black rayon machine-embroidery thread in the needle and black all-purpose thread in the bobbin, machine-stitch around stars with a narrow zigzag stitch.

Step 8. Make narrow hem in long, bordered edge and both short ends of skirt. Gather remaining long edge, evenly adjusting gathers around skirt. Pin skirt to bodice and stitch; press. ✽

**My Buddy 'N' Me
Doll Jumper Bodice Front**
Cut 2 primary fabric
(reverse 1)
Cut 2 trim fabric
(reverse 1)

Center front line

**My Buddy 'N' Me
Child Jumper Stars**
Cut 15 yellow

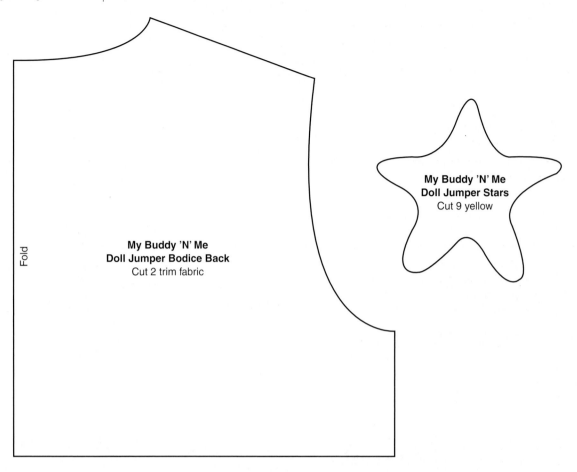

My Buddy 'N' Me
Doll Jumper Bodice Back
Cut 2 trim fabric

Fold

My Buddy 'N' Me
Doll Jumper Stars
Cut 9 yellow

Lace Medallion Bible Cover

Continued from page 168

Step 5. Cut two pieces each cover fabric, lining and batting 4" wide by the cut height of the Bible cover. Sandwich the layers, lining and cover fabric right sides together. Sew down one long side of each layered set. Turn lining back and press.

Step 6. From cover fabric cut two strips 1½" x 10" for handles. Fold lengthwise, right sides together, and sew long edge. Turn right side out and press. Pin ends to right and left sides of cover, aligning raw edges.

Step 7. Place pieces made in Step 5 right sides together with main cover, aligning outer and top and bottom edges. Place lining piece right sides together with cover and sew around perimeter leaving an opening for turning. Turn right side out. Hand-stitch opening closed.

Step 8. Hand-stitch loose side of back pocket in place. Stitch medallion and flower to front cover. Slide book covers into inside pockets. ✻

BASIC INSTRUCTIONS

Basic Sewing Supplies

- Sewing machine
- Sharp scissors or shears
- Straight pins
- Hand-sewing needles
- Thimble (optional)
- Seam ripper
- Chalk marker or fade-out pen (for temporary marks)

An iron and ironing board, although not strictly sewing tools, are essential to great-looking projects. Don't be afraid to use them liberally!

HANDMADE STITCHES

Buttonhole Stitch

(Sometimes called blanket stitch)

Working left to right, bring needle up at A, down at B and up at C with thread below needle. Stitches should be evenly spaced and of a consistent depth.

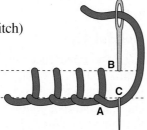

French Knot

Bring the needle up through the fabric. Point the needle at yourself, then wrap the thread or floss clockwise around the needle. Insert the needle back down through the fabric one thread away from the exit point.

Lazy-Daisy Stitch

Bring needle up through fabric at A, make a loop and hold it with your thumb. Insert the needle back down through fabric at A and up at B. Make a small anchor stitch to hold the loop in place.

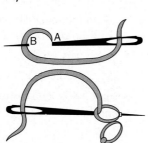

Slip-Stitch

Slip-stitching is worked by hand to make an almost invisible finish.

1. Work with a single thread along two folded edges.

2. Insert needle in one fold and slide a short distance.

3. Pick up a thread from the other folded edge and slip point of needle back in first fold.

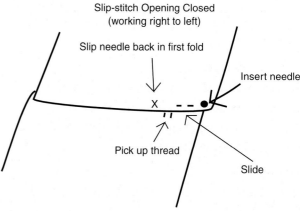

Slip-stitch Opening Closed
(working right to left)

Slip needle back in first fold

Insert needle

X

Pick up thread

Slide

4. Repeat (slide, pick up thread, insert back in first fold) along length of opening.

5. Bury knot between folds.

Straight Stitch

The basis of many hand-embroidery stitches, the straight stitch is formed by bringing the needle up at A and down at B.

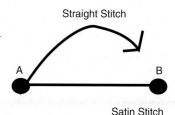

Straight Stitch

A   B

Satin Stitch

Satin stitches are simply straight stitches worked very closely together to fill in a solid shape. That shape is sometimes outlined for additional definition. *Note: Threads should lie closely side by side, but not overlapping.*

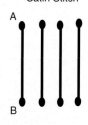

Satin Stitch

A

B

ENLARGING PATTERNS

There are several ways to enlarge patterns—all of which are perfectly acceptable. Please choose the method that works best for you.

Photocopy

Photocopy the pattern provided at a copy shop at the percentage enlargement you want (100 percent is the size of the original; 150 percent is 1½ times the original; 200 percent is twice the size of the original, etc). If the shopkeeper objects, due to copyright infringement, tell him you have permission from the publisher to make one copy so you don't have to cut the book (show him this note, if necessary).

Grid Pattern

Any pattern can also be enlarged using a grid pattern.

Draw a grid on the pattern every ½". Then, draw 1" grid on a piece of tracing paper or other lightweight paper. The final step is to transfer the lines in each grid from the pattern to the 1" grid. This is equal to photo-copying the pattern at 200 percent.

TRANSFERRING PATTERNS

There are several methods for transferring pattern out-lines and details. Choose the one that works best for your project.

Outline Pattern

1. Place tracing paper over pattern in book or magazine.

2. Trace with pencil; cut out with scissors.

3. Place pattern on the project. Pin in place, then cut or draw around the periphery.

Graphite Paper

When details need to be transferred as well as the pattern outline:

1. Place tracing paper over pattern in book or magazine.

2. Trace with pencil, but do not cut out.

3. Place pattern on the project; insert graphite or trans-fer paper between the project and pattern with the media side toward the fabric.

4. Retrace design lines with a dried-out ball point pen to transfer lines to fabric.

Iron-on Transfer Pencil

Another method for transferring pattern details:

1. Place tracing paper over pattern in book or magazine.

2. Trace with pencil, but do not cut out.

3. Turn paper over; trace detail lines with an iron-on transfer pencil.

4. Place pattern on the project with the media side toward the fabric.

5. Apply heat with an iron, following manufacturer's directions to transfer marks to fabric.

SATIN STITCH BY MACHINE

Machine-made satin stitches are often used to finish appliqué pieces and consist of closely worked zig-zag stitches.

Stitch Size

The width and length of the stitches are determined by the size of the appliqué and the body of the fabric.

1. Small appliqué pieces call for narrow zigzag stitches.

2. Large appliqué pieces call for wider zigzag stitches.

3. Fragile or brittle fabrics, such as metallics, lamés, sheer organza, etc., require longer stitches to prevent damaging fibers and effectively "cutting"

the appliqué piece out of the background.

4. Fuzzy fabrics, such as shaggy felt or synthetic fur, require wider stitches and a medium width.

Threads

Threads used for satin-stitch appliqué are chosen for their weight, color and finish.

1. For fine fabrics, those with small woven threads, choose a fine thread, such as silk, rayon, or thin cotton. Machine embroidery threads are a good choice.

2. For medium-weight fabrics, a medium-weight rayon or cotton thread works nicely. Threads in variegated colors add interest.

3. Heavy-weight fabrics might do well with a heavy-duty thread worked in a buttonhole stitch, rather than satin stitch.

4. Test threads of different weights and finishes on a sample of the fabrics in your project before making the final choice.

5. Select threads in coordinating or contrasting colors, as desired.

Helpful Tips

1. Thread upper machine with rayon thread and bobbin with a cotton or cotton-wrapped polyester thread in a color neutral to the backing, if the back will show. Or, chose a cotton or cotton-wrapped polyester thread in the same color used on the top if the backing will not be visible in the completed project.

2. Loosen the top tension slightly. This pulls the loop of the stitch to the back for a smooth look on the top.

3. When turning inside corners, stop with the needle down in the fabric on the inside (see Fig. 1).

4. When turning outside corners, stop with the needle down in the fabric on the outside (see Fig. 2).

5. If the machine is skipping stitches:

- Clean the machine thoroughly, removing any build-up of fuzz beneath the feed dogs.
- Use a new needle.
- Try a needle of a different size.
- Match size and point of needle to the thread and fabric in the project.

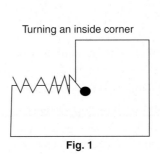

Turning an inside corner

Fig. 1

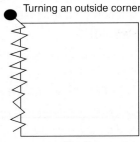

Turning an outside corner

Fig. 2

- Apply a silicone needle lubricant to the needle, thread, and every place the thread touches the machine in the upper threading track.

6. An iron-on, tear-away stabilizer seems like an unnecessary purchase, but what it adds to the quality of a machine-appliquéd project cannot be denied. The product is ironed on the wrong side of the fabric under the area to be appliquéd. This keeps it from shifting during machine-stitching. When the work is done, the stabilizer is simply torn away. A touch of the iron adds the finishing touch for an appliqué project free of lumps and bumps!

TEA-DYING FABRIC

Fabric can be dyed in a bath of strong tea to give it an aged effect.

1. Wet the fabric in clear water; squeeze excess moisture from fabric, but do not wring or twist.

2. Immerse in a hot bath of water and several tea bags. Allow to soak for 20–30 minutes.

3. Remove fabric; squeeze excess moisture out.

4. Hang fabric to dry, or dry in dryer.

Helpful Tips

- Fabric will dry lighter than it appears when wet.
- Conservationists warn that tannic acid in such a tea bath will cause damage to fabrics over a period of years, so this method should not be used on an heirloom project.
- 100-percent cotton muslin or broadcloth works best.

GATHERING STITCHES BY HAND

Work a long running stitch close to the edge of the piece to be gathered with a doubled thread. Pull gently to gather. If fabric is heavy, use heavy-duty thread, such as carpet thread.

GATHERING STITCHES BY MACHINE

To work gathering stitches by machine, set the sewing machine for the longest stitch possible (some newer machines have a built-in basting stitch). Pull the bobbin thread firmly and evenly to gather.

If the fabric is heavy, work a medium zigzag stitch over a strand of thin crochet thread. Then, pull the crochet thread to gather.

TOPSTITCHING TRIMS BY MACHINE

Rickrack

To attach narrow rickrack by machine, run a straight stitch down the center of the trim. To attach wide rickrack, work a zigzag stitch or a broken zigzag along length of the trim.

Piping

To attach piping, baste close to the piping (use a zipper foot, if necessary) on one piece of the project with raw edges even. Place the other piece on the project, with right sides together, and stitch along the basting stitches through all layers of the project.

Cording

To attach cording or other narrow trims, work a zigzag stitch slightly wider than the trim with monofilament thread (for an invisible stitch) or with decorative threads for an embellished look.

USING FUSIBLE WEB

There is more than one kind of fusible web! The light or ultra-light versions have less adhesive on them and will accept machine stitches. The heavy-duty versions have a thicker layer of adhesive and are designed to be used without machine stitches. In fact, if you try to sew through the heavy-duty kind, the adhesive gums up the needle and causes a mess.

The best advice is to read the manufacturer's directions. Each manufacturer has a different formula for the adhesive and may require different handling.

Regardless of the type fusible product you choose, they may all be applied to fabric in generally the same way.

Fusible Appliqué

1. Trace the desired motif on paper side of the adhesive with a marking tool (pen, pencil, permanent marker, etc.).

2. Cut out around the marks, leaving a margin.

3. Bond the fusible webbing to the wrong side of desired fabric.

4. Cut through fabric, webbing and paper backing, following the drawn shape.

5. Remove paper backing and place the shape on desired background.

6. Fuse in place, following manufacturer's directions.

7. Finish edges with machine-worked stitches or fabric paint, if desired. ❦

SPECIAL THANKS

We would like to thank the talented designers whose work is featured in this collection.

Mary Ayres
Buttoned-Up Ornaments
Ice Crystal Ornament
Reindeer Bib

Joanne Bembry
Holiday Hostess Apron

Nancy Brenan Daniel
Patchwork Petals Tree Skirt
Folk Santa Doll

Kathy Brown
Christmas Card Envelope
Kitty & Doggie Bibs

Julie DeGroat
Melt-Your-Heart Snowmen
  Ornaments
L'il Bear Hugs Teddy Bear

Phyllis M. Dobbs
Gingerbread Ornaments
Fluffy Snowmen
Poinsettia Hot Mats
Country Angel Christmas
  Stocking
Elegant Tasseled Mantel
  Scarf
Moonlight Trees
  Centerpiece
Wee Santa Shelf Sitter

Pat Everson
Christmas Wrap Organizer

June Fiechter
Gilded Stars Tree Skirt
Christmas Kitty Draft
  Catcher
Gingerbread Grins Pillow
Tumbling Stars Place Mat
  Set
Snowy, Snowy Night
  Sweatshirts
Holly Buttons Christmas
  Outfit
Trio of Trees Dress
Angel Tree Topper

Donna Friebertshauser
Elegant Ornaments
Holiday Sparkle Jewelry Set

Lee Lindeman
Flying Santa Wind Sock
Blustery Snowman
  Wind Sock

Janice Loewenthal
Season's Greetings Mailbox
  Cover
Gingergread Placemat and
  Napkin Keeper

Twinkle, Twinkle Little
  Angel Vest

Chris Malone
Angel Garland
Peek-a-Boo Gift Bags
Country Christmas Hearts
  Valance
Here Comes Santa Pillow
Teacher's Helper Doll

Connie Matricardi
Star Baby Beanbags
Christmas Elves Shelf
  Sitters
Christmas Topiary Stocking
Tumbling Snowmen Vest
Pin Pillows
Christmas Puppets

Janice McKee
Crazy Quilt Treasure Box

Karen Mead
Hallelujah Angel Pin
Winter Silhouettes

Karen Neary
Easy Cutwork Snowflakes
  Ornaments
Cutwork Snowflakes Mantel
  Scarf

Jill Reber
Holly Dreams Sheet Set

Marian Shenk
Doggie Treats Stocking
Dapper Snowman Stocking
Daddy's Old Ties Clutch
  Purse
Lace Medallion Bible Cover

Charlyne Stewart
Twinkling Star Place Mats
Poinsettia Cobbler Apron

Norma Storm
Log Cabin Angels

Barbara E. Swanson
The Heart of Christmas
Holiday Cheer Stationery
  Set
Christmas Tic-Tac-Toe

Julie Weaver
Snowmen on Parade
Holiday Holly Vest
Toasty Warm Snowman

Beth Wheeler
My Buddy 'N' Me Jumpers